RECLAIMING OUR PRODIGAL SONS AND DAUGHTERS

A Practical Approach for Connecting With Youth in Conflict

Scott Larson
Larry Brendtro

National Educational Service
Bloomington, Indiana   2000

Cover illustration by Maureen Pesta

Cover design by Grannan Graphics

Printed in the United States of America

ISBN 1-879639-69-6

Dedication

*To the children we have parented
and to those we have reparented.*

Contents

Part Two: The Road Home

Foreword

Lively and jargon-free, *Reclaiming Our Prodigal Sons and Daughters* blends the wisdom of great youth pioneers with the best research on positive youth development. This book also makes a strong case that, unless we nurture the spiritual dimension of young people, we fail to meet all of their needs. Moving stories of young people struggling to rebuild their lives are used to illustrate key strategies for replacing pessimism with a spirit of hope.

The timing for such a book could not be better. There is a growing concern that something is wrong with a society that produces so many unconnected youth. Many of today's educational and treatment systems actually discourage teachers, counselors, and youthworkers from forming close attachments with the youth they serve. But without positive bonds to adults, children often lack a moral compass. Connecting with youth must be a shared endeavor involving families, schools, youth professionals, neighborhood leaders, and members of the faith community.

The authors bring an unusual depth and diversity of experience to *Reclaiming Our Prodigal Sons and Daughters*, drawing from a combined 60 years of work with challenging youth. Dr. Larson is a prominent leader in youth ministry who has published widely on the spiritual development of youth at risk. Throughout his long professional career, Dr. Brendtro has counseled thousands of youth—from runaways to violent teenagers. The synergy of their collaboration has produced a powerful, practical plan for reclaiming today's troubled children and youth.

—Arlin E. Ness
President, Starr Commonwealth

Part One

Our
Wayward
Youth

CHAPTER 1

Hazards in the World of Children

growing up in the twenty-first century

When the young generation is inspired with the feeling of having great acts to do, a new century begins.
—Ellen Key, Swedish sociologist (1900)

THE TWENTIETH CENTURY opened with a spirit of great optimism about the futures of youth. Many sociologists and psychologists predicted that science and technology were about to create *the century of the child*. But the 1900s would end with a rash of youth violence and school killings that threatened not only children of poverty, but also children of privilege. How could a century that began with such optimism end so despairingly?

Before the twentieth century, wayward youth were given the same harsh penalties as adults, locked away in prisons and poorhouses or even executed. But in 1899, a group of remarkable midwestern women, working with the Chicago Bar Association, created the world's first juvenile court. From its inception, its goal was to reclaim—rather than to discard—our most needy and troubled children.

Who would have predicted that a century later hundreds of thousands of children would be locked away in adult prisons and detention centers, giving the United States the highest incarceration rate of teens in the world? Amidst a furious debate over what went wrong, citizens worldwide would enter the twenty-first century fearing for the futures of their children.

The Origins of the Dilemma

Our present-day crisis dates back at least 100 years to the time when adolescence, as a term and concept, was invented. Prior to the industrial revolution, it was necessary that everyone in the family, from age 5 up, work. Some cooked, some cared for younger siblings, and others labored in the family business. Interactions with adults of all ages were natural and the norm in areas of work, school, sports, and leisure. The transition from childhood to adulthood was relatively smooth, as young people were naturally apprenticed into the adult world of work and responsibility.

But with the dawn of industrialization, modern society began segregating young people from the world of adults. Work was removed from the home, and child labor laws were created in response to the abuse of children in "sweat factories." The net result was that youth were kept out of the workforce entirely. At the same time, the creation of compulsory education required children to attend formalized schools, where they were segregated into age-specific groups. Adults assumed more "professional roles" such as educators and therapists and, in effect, distanced themselves from the intimate contact with youth that had always been the norm.

Beginning in 1890, scientists began formulating the concept of *adolescence*. Psychologist G. Stanley Hall was one of the first to popularize the theory that sexual maturation was the most significant thing going on in the life of a young person. As a result, a natural biological process of maturation would define an entire age group, setting it apart from all others. Sigmund Freud described adolescence as a kind of stress disorder triggered by sexual urges, and Anna Freud stated that normality during this period was itself an abnormal state of affairs.

A New Type of Adolescent

Teenagers of the twenty-first century are worlds apart from the youth of a century earlier or from those being raised in more traditional cultures. Though we may try to shelter our youth from modern culture, its influence cannot be denied. The three major shifts discussed below have led to modern adolescence over the past 100 years.

Segregated From the World of Adults

As informal child-rearing systems declined, formal youth organizations emerged. Thus, in the twentieth century, a whole array of adult institutions was launched to help segregate and protect youth from adult stress while they matured. The scouting movement, age-graded high schools, and organized sports were all created with the sole purpose of socializing youth, a process that had always occurred quite naturally in earlier generations and continues still in more tribal communities.

Instead of having youth do real work because their labor was needed, chores were invented for them with the purpose of teaching them responsibility, helpfulness, order, and unselfishness. But pseudo-work does not develop character. In fact, it generally does the opposite. Would you be motivated to go to a job every day if you knew your work had no real value but was invented solely to help you develop character?

Today the majority of young people do not have to work for basic sustenance of themselves or their families. Although many teens hold jobs, they often use their considerable earnings purely to subsidize materialistic lifestyles.

The net effect of all of this was the creation of a subculture called *adolescence*. The twenty-first century is now experiencing the full definition of what was created in the previous century: the concept that sexuality and social life dominate what it means to be adolescent. And adolescents have lived up to our expectations, though we would now desperately like to change that.[1]

Raised in a Spiritual Vacuum

In 1900, the famous Swedish sociologist Ellen Key enthusiastically trumpeted *the century of the child*. Although she had many creative ideas, Key was a strident critic of religious faith, viewing it as something that contributed to the problems of youth. She saw religion as little more than antiquated myths that would be swept away by a new commitment to science and the humanistic ethic. Her view reflected the convictions of many in the emerging child-care profession, making controversies about religion common in the twentieth century. As a result, most educators and clinicians chose to avoid spiritual issues.

Yet throughout history, most societies have held spiritual truths in highest esteem, ensuring that they are passed on from generation to generation. In the mid-1900s, Holocaust survivor and psychologist Viktor Frankl lamented how psychiatry had virtually ignored the spiritual dimension in those it was attempting to treat. He challenged the psychological concepts that were based on the idea that life was little more than the quest for self-gratification. Sigmund Freud believed the pursuit of pleasure was the central human motivation, and Alfred Adler argued that it was the struggle for power that motivated people. But Frankl pointed out that they both worked mainly with sick patients, and that pleasure and power were but shallow substitutes for the failure to find spiritual meaning.

Nonetheless, as the fields of education, corrections, and psychology attempted to become more scientific, moral and spiritual issues were pushed aside. The result was a century-long social experiment in operating a secular society cut adrift from spiritual moorings.

Nurtured by the Media

With the diminished influence of extended families, communities, and churches, great stress was placed on the isolated nuclear family. This is not just a problem of disadvantaged or single-parent families. Rampant materialism may be the most serious new threat to children. As Ellen Key had warned a century earlier, parents who are obsessed with obtaining wealth will raise degenerate children as surely as if the parents were addicted to alcohol or opium.

Ours may be the first generation growing up without the eyes of adults upon them. Without adult attachments, bonds to peers are much stronger than in cultures where families still raise the children. But when the primary source of values comes from the youth subculture itself, children are left without a moral compass.

Into this values void moves the entertainment industry with its willingness to provide the road maps for children who do not receive them from home, schools, or churches. But the relationship between youth and the media is symbiotic. Not only does the media need the billions of dollars young people spend on entertainment, but youth are also turning to the media for nurturing and guidance. Sixteen-year-old Dustin described to us his attachment to music:

> If you relate to these people, the music they sing will have a greater effect on you. I have listened to their music for the last few years, and it seems like they are singing about me and the situations in my life. I know a lot of kids who use music as a counselor or therapist. Some music has a negative effect, like songs about killing your mom, killing your dad, killing God, and eventually killing yourself. But some songs are about how to make it through life even if you were dealt a bad hand.
>
> My favorite musician is Jonathan Davis, who is lead singer in the band known as koRn. As a young kid he grew up abused and neglected and is now trying to make something out of his life. These people affect my life a lot. They show me that even [though] I didn't grow up the best way, I can still make my life into something.

Youth in Conflict

While many youth manage to navigate through adolescence relatively unscathed, others are deeply wounded by their experiences. Some internalize their pain while others act out in more destructive ways. In the past, privileged communities were able to insulate themselves from the effects of juvenile crime. But juvenile crime follows the path of most youth trends, beginning in our inner cities 10 to 15 years before they are commonplace in our suburbs and rural communities. Today, violence is a mainstream problem in middle- and upper-class neighborhoods throughout America.

After the Columbine High School massacre in 1999, many adults found it hard to understand how youth in good neighborhoods would even think of killing one another. But the hundreds of copycat threats of violence that were made in the months that followed demonstrated how this tragic act of retribution had resonated with thousands of youth whose own fury was bottled up inside.

A week after the Columbine shootings, a North Dakota student named Richard Fransen expressed the feelings of so many frustrated teens in a letter to the editor:

> Between grades seven and nine, I was one of those kids that everyone picked on. I was an easy target, I had few friends and for three years, I absolutely dreaded the seven hours a day that I had to be in school. The work itself was no problem. I had nearly a 4.0, but as I'm sure everyone knows, kids that age are extremely cruel to those who are too shy and insecure to fight back. For three years I endured almost constant heckling, book dumpings, and I was hit on numerous occasions.
>
> I can vividly remember many walks to school each morning trying to concoct a plan to either kill myself or those assholes who never let me be. The only thing that ever stopped me was that I could not work up the guts to actually do it. I'm 22 years old now, but I have no doubt that what happened in Colorado last week could have easily happened here in Grand Forks by my hand. And I'm sure it's only a matter of time before some 15-year-old comes along who has the guts to use a gun to take care of the problems that the teachers and other faculty members had been completely oblivious to.[2]

When young people think such thoughts, it frightens all of us. The rage, vengeance, and nihilism of many contemporary youth is a testament to lives without spiritual purpose. How do we make sense of what appears to be such senseless and self-defeating behavior? Will we reach out to hurting and hating teens in our schools, courts, churches, and communities, or will we discard them? And what do young people need from us as they seek to find purpose and meaning in their lives?

We enter a new century asking age-old questions. Have we learned from the mistakes of the past so we can avoid repeating them? Are we ready to rediscover and apply those enduring truths that have sustained us for so long? Such questions are the focus of this book.

But before we probe further into the uniqueness of contemporary youth, we first go back 2,000 years to the parable of the prodigal son. It is an account of a rebellious youth who turns his back on the values of his family, wasting his life in a futile pursuit of pleasure through wild and self-destructive living. But more important, the parable is a story of redemption and restoration. Hidden within it is an enduring paradigm that must be rediscovered and reapplied if we are to positively impact the troubled youth in our own lives. Our willingness to grapple honestly with these issues may determine our future in the new millennium more than anything else we do.

CHAPTER 2

Reclaiming a Prodigal
a parable for our times

I wanted to be free by cutting myself off from my father and my roots. Fool that I am! I have found nothing but chains.

—Helmut Thielicke, German theologian (1908–1986)

WHILE THERE ARE DEEPLY TROUBLED CHILDREN in every community, most of us do not encounter them. Yet we all share the same fears: Will our children be led astray by negative peers? Will they use drugs, drink alcohol, or engage in other risky behavior? Will they have difficulties with teachers or break the law? What if they reject the values we hold dear? Most adults feel powerless when they consider the many temptations that confront their children. In spite of our best efforts and intentions, even children raised in the best of homes can go astray.

The Prodigal Son

This was the case in the parable of the prodigal son as told by Jesus in the 15th chapter of Luke. This timeless parable provides us with a fresh understanding of how we can reclaim wayward youth, regardless of the cause of their dilemma.

A Parable of Reclaiming

There was a man who had two sons. The younger of them said to his father, "Father, give me the share of the property that will belong to me." So he divided his property between them. A few days later the younger son gathered all he had and traveled to a distant country, and there he squandered his property in dissolute living.

When he had spent everything, a severe famine took place throughout that country, and he began to be in need. So he went and hired himself out to one of the citizens of that country, who sent him to his fields to feed the pigs. He would gladly have filled himself with the pods that the pigs were eating; and no one gave him anything.

But when he came to himself he said, "How many of my father's hired hands have bread enough and to spare, but here I am dying of hunger! I will get up and go to my father, and I will say to him, 'Father, I have sinned against heaven and before you; I am no longer worthy to be called your son; treat me like one of your hired hands.'"

So he set off and went to his father. But while he was still far off, his father saw him and was filled with compassion; he ran and put his arms around him and kissed him. Then the son said to him, "Father, I have sinned against heaven and before you; I am no longer worthy to be called your son."

But the father said to his slaves, "Quickly, bring out a robe—the best one—and put it on him; put a ring on his finger and sandals on his feet. And get the fatted calf and kill it, and let us eat and celebrate; for this son of mine was dead and is alive again; he was lost and is found!" And they began to celebrate.

Now his elder son was in the field; and when he came and approached the house, he heard music and dancing. He called one of the slaves and asked what was going on. He replied, "Your brother has come, and your father has killed the fatted calf, because he has got him back safe and sound." Then he became angry and refused to go in. His father came out and began to plead with him.

But he answered his father, "Listen! For all these years I have been working like a slave for you, and I have never disobeyed your command; yet you have never given me even a young goat so that I might celebrate with my friends. But when this son of yours came back, who has devoured your property with prostitutes, you killed the fatted calf for him!"

Then the father said to him, "Son, you are always with me, and all that is mine is yours. But we had to celebrate and rejoice, because this brother of yours was dead and has come to life; he was lost and has been found."

—Luke 15:11–32 (NRSV)

One of the most poignant commentaries on the parable of the prodigal son comes from the sermons of German theologian Helmut Thielicke. Still in his 20s, he became a professor at the University of Heidelberg where he spoke out boldly against Hitler. He toured the country expounding the Gospel until, like Dietrich Bonhoeffer and other courageous pastors, he was forbidden to travel or speak publicly. During this time, Thielicke's sermons were secretly transcribed and distributed throughout the country. One of the most popular was titled, "The Waiting Father." We borrow from Thielicke's style and substance in our discussion of the parable, rephrasing his sermon in the language of our own time.

The Search for Freedom

This prodigal son did not run from an abusive or neglectful or impoverished home. His was a loving family. With so much going for him, why would this son make such a bold, ludicrous demand for his share of the inheritance before his father had even died? Or perhaps more shocking, why would his father honor it?

In traditional Middle Eastern cultures, such a request would be unthinkable, evoking anger and swift punishment from any father, for the son is in essence saying, "You're as good as dead to me, dad. I don't want to wait until you're gone to get what is rightfully mine. I want it now!"

Nevertheless, this father grants the request. It means, however, that he must sell half of his estate; as the New English Bible puts it, "He gathered all he had and turned [it] into cash." Such an act would also cut the father's ability to produce income in half.

What would possess a child to make such a bold request? Had he been spoiled and pampered, growing accustomed to always getting his own way? Perhaps he was fed up with being the baby of the family and wanted to be his own man: "Everybody's always telling me what to do! The old man is getting on my nerves. I'm bored to death! I can't take it anymore!" Perhaps he had heard peers from less-privileged backgrounds tell raucous stories, which fed his hunger for freedom: "Drugs, women, life on the road. These guys can do what they want, but I'm stuck in this boring place!"

"Father, I want my freedom. You're always telling me what to do. You treat me like a little boy, and I'm almost a man." The father tried to explain how much he loved his son, which was why he had given him limits. In the end, they were at an impasse in their concepts of freedom. Freedom to the son meant "I should be able to do whatever I want." To the father, it meant "You should become what you were meant to be."

As caregivers, we are never quite sure how best to help children grow into healthy adults. Letting them run free only yields spoiled brats. Keeping them tightly controlled turns them into cowards or rebels. Where is the middle ground?

The biggest transformation with the onset of adolescence is the lust for freedom. Nearly every young person struggles in this passage, but most do so without disaster. But when youthful autonomy battles with adult authority, we call it rebellion. Some teens just will not be told what to do. When they get something in their minds, there is just no stopping them. And so it was with the prodigal son who set out on his search for freedom and independence—dependent on his dad's money, of course.

The Powerlessness of Parents

The departure is not a pleasant scene. After a hurried sale of the estate, within only a few days the son is gone. The text does not indicate that the son embraces his parents or even says, "Thank you and good-bye." Instead, he gathers up all his possessions and is gone. He leaves nothing behind because he is not planning to return: "I'm out of here. Look out world, here I come!" As the son sets out chasing after thrills, he is oblivious to what lies ahead. But the father is wiser in the ways of the world, and he fears the worst. He knows what hazards face an immature, impulsive, self-centered son who will not listen to anybody.

We know what must have been going on in the hearts and minds of the parents. Their youngest child had turned his back on them. "Where have we gone wrong?" they must wonder. Every step causes pain. They try to get on with their lives, but they cannot keep him from their thoughts. Even his empty place at the table reminds them of his absence.

If these parents had searched the Torah seeking comfort, they would have found many stories of battles between boys and fathers. Most do not have happy endings. David's sons turned out to be a rogue's gallery of criminals that included a murderer and a rapist. Aaron was a priest, but two of his sons lost their lives because of their sin. "Will tragedy come to our son as well?" the parents wonder. They tell themselves he is in God's hands, but all the while they fear he is going to the devil. Day after day there is no news. They feel powerless. What can they do, but pray and watch and wait?

The Wayward Son

The father's fears are well founded. Uprooted in a far country, the son uses his money to find new friends and joins up with others who, like him, are adrift. Runaways and outcasts, unguided and unattached, they are free to do whatever they want. So they plunge headlong into wild living, drunkenness, and sexual promiscuity. For a while, he forgets about home, but when the parties are over, he feels desperately alone.

Children who are spiritually empty cannot stand the quiet because they do not want to be alone with their thoughts. They attempt to cover the emptiness with noise and wild celebration. This prodigal pursues any type of diversion. His urges, his loneliness, and his passions bind him until he is no longer free. Still, a front conceals his unhappiness from his peers. For a time, he pretends that his gang is his family, but he knows it is a cheap substitute. His celebrations become stale; his money runs out. His "friends" leave him. He feels the pains of starvation in his heart as well as in his belly.

When he hits bottom, his world collapses, and he is overwhelmed by feelings of depression and disgust. In the silence of the night, he hears his father's voice in his mind and recalls the memory of his mother in his heart. Sometimes he dreams he is back home but awakens to find he is still far away. He wonders what he might say to his parents if he were to go back.

Such reminiscing reminds him where he really belongs. He is more fortunate than some of his associates who never knew their fathers and who have been on the run for years. There can be no going home without a home.

He can still hear the voice of his conscience, instilled in him as a small boy. He knows he has terribly disappointed his parents and caused them great pain. Is he genuinely remorseful? We do not know. Only one thing is certain: He is hungry.

The young lad believes that being reinstated as a son is impossible. Even his father's hired hands have bread to eat, and he is starving! But he needs more than just physical sustenance. He is broken. More than just food, he desires forgiveness and a chance to say, "I was wrong. I'm sorry."

The son rehearses a speech in his mind as he starts back home. He is as fearful of the people in the village as he is of facing his parents. He knows the dreaded "qetsateh ceremony" is the punishment for any Jewish boy who dares to come home after losing the family inheritance to Gentiles.[1] In this ritual of banishment, his former neighbors would bring a large jar filled with burned corn and nuts, breaking the items in front of him while shouting, "You are forever cut off from your people!" From then on, they would have nothing to do with him. In spite of this impending humiliation, he heads home.

The Homecoming

When we last left the father, he was waiting and watching, so he is the first to see the boy from afar. He is also well aware of the impending qetsateh ceremony and begins running to the boy. To run clothed in a long robe is a dishonoring sight for any Middle Eastern patriarch. But run the father does, for he must intercept the villagers before they begin the banishment ritual.

When the father and son meet, the father does not even wait to hear his son's explanation. Instead he embraces him, ready to forgive before an apology is tendered. Some fathers might have blamed: "You've certainly made a mess of things." Some fathers might have shamed: "Well, I hope you've learned your lesson." But this father just could not wait to give his son a hug. The most powerful of all spiritual transactions has occurred. The father forgives fully, no strings attached.

Forgiveness, of course, does not negate consequences. The son would never be able to get back those years he had lost, and his inheritance was gone forever. All that his father owned would now go only to his brother. But his sonship was never in question—a gift beyond his wildest hopes.

Once absolution was given, the celebration could begin. Whatever resources were at hand were showered on the son. Though he does not deserve this outpouring of love, the son's return mattered more than the record of his wrongs.

A great miracle happened. The lost son returned home, and now he is free—free to enjoy again the status of being a son and free from the urges, loneliness, and passions that had once bound him. It is a time of great joy, and the father exclaims, "Let us eat and celebrate for this son of mine was dead and is alive again; he was lost and is found!"

To Hate or to Forgive?

The elder son is infuriated when he hears the music and dancing, for he cannot believe his ears. The sight of his brother conjures up waves of repugnance and reproach, not compassion. He refuses to even claim him. Rather than "*My brother* is back," he says with disgust: "*This son of yours* came back!"

"He is not worth wasting money on," he complains bitterly to his father. "Why should my inheritance be used to subsidize this vagabond?" So he shuns his brother, refusing to join in the celebration. He wants him to remain an outcast.

At the end of the story, we are left with yet another conflict between father and son. Now the elder brother is no longer free. In walking away from the family celebration, he has estranged himself as surely as his younger brother once had done.

The parable of this prodigal son is above all a testament to the miracle of forgiveness. It was told to highly judgmental Pharisees who were offended when Jesus fraternized with blatant sinners. It is part of a trilogy of short stories about a lost sheep, a lost coin, and finally a lost son. Each story ends with a celebration, for a possession of great worth has been recovered. There is no greater joy than when a prodigal is reclaimed. This parable echoes the prophetic words from the prophet Zechariah, written hundreds of years before:

> Take off his dirty clothes and dress him in splendid robes and put a turban on his head. So they put a turban on his head and dressed him in clean clothes while the angel of Yahweh stood by and said, "You see I have taken your guilt away."[2]

Pioneers in Reclaiming Prodigals

The word *reclaim* appears only once in the Bible, though it is a major theme of the scriptures. In the 11th chapter of Isaiah, the prophet speaks of a time when the Messiah will come and *reclaim* his people, bringing the outcasts home from the far corners of the earth. In this time, the wolf will dwell peaceably with the lamb, and the world will be made safe for the young. Even the smallest and most vulnerable child will be sheltered from harm, protected under a banner of love.

Reclaiming lost youth has a long and rich tradition. For more than 200 years, pioneers in youth work, driven by strong spiritual convictions, have reached out to those others have pushed away. As we seek answers to today's youth problems, we might recall the observation of the German poet Goethe: "Everything important has been thought of before. The difficulty is to think of it again." Early pioneers in youth work radiated an optimism in the face of pessimistic approaches that focused only on the negative traits of troubled teens. By challenging society's attitudes of futility and cynicism, these pioneers proved that even the most difficult children can be reclaimed.

Johann Heinrich Pestalozzi (1746–1827) of Switzerland was the founder of enlightened approaches to helping troubled children. He welcomed outcast youth who roamed the streets after the Napoleonic wars. In his castle school, he replaced flogging with correction through kindness, challenging those who saw little worth in these wild children. Pestalozzi declared that "It is vain to say to the orphan, 'You have a father in heaven.' But if you bring up the little orphan as if he had a father, you teach him to know his Father in Heaven."[3]

In the United States, Dorothea Dix (1802–1887) was shocked at conditions she discovered as a Sunday school teacher for female prisoners. She awakened a nation's conscience to the plight of troubled persons, including young children locked away in almshouses and stables. She sparked a worldwide crusade to save society's emotionally wounded.

Father Don Bosco (1815–1888) of Italy developed his "preventive system" that was based on corrective adult mentoring as an alternative to repressive punishment. Today, Salesian priests continue his efforts through a worldwide network of programs for youth of the streets. These programs welcome those turned away by other agencies—"throw-away kids" who were prisoners of sexual abuse, drugs, or crime.

In the early nineteenth century in England, teenager George Mueller (1805–1898) was imprisoned for thievery. But, through a friend, he heard the message of God's love for him, and his life changed completely. Later, he became a pastor. Mueller's concern for the plight of the orphans in Bristol motivated him to start five separate orphanages that would support more than 10,000 orphans during his lifetime.

Bengali poet Rabindranath Tagore won the Nobel Prize in 1915 for his poetry about children. As head of a school for cast-off street children in Bolpur, India, he worked with youth who were struggling to find purpose for their lives. He writes, "When the heart despairs of finding water, it is easy enough to be deluded by a mirage and driven in barren quest from desert to desert."[4]

With the dawn of the twentieth century, progressive approaches to delinquents sprang up worldwide. Jane Addams (1860–1935), also a Nobel Peace Prize winner, developed programs for kids who were involved in the gangs of Chicago—youth whose easy access to drugs and guns triggered violence like that of today. She recognized that the real solution to delinquency was not in the courts, but in communities where caring adults would pass on enduring values. She challenged churches, synagogues, and schools to nurture character in needy youth. She believed that when adults became moral teachers, they would tap the latent idealism of youth.

Led by Jane Addams, the juvenile court system in the United States was established in 1899 and soon was adopted by virtually all democratic nations. The guiding doctrine was *parens patriae.* This theory recognized that youth were not simply short adults or even young adults—they had needs distinctive to their developmental stages and were uniquely reclaimable.

In 1925, delinquency pioneer August Aichorn (1878–1949) of Austria wrote the book *Wayward Youth.* He had worked directly with delinquents for decades and rejected both punitiveness and sentimentalism. The primary unmet need of most delinquents was love, he believed. This need was seldom met because their behavior elicited punishment, which only fueled their distrust of adult authority. Permissiveness also failed, for delinquents would only take advantage of sympathetic adults they saw as weak. The challenge was to develop new ways of connecting to children who refused to be loved.

It is notable that, given its roots in the Torah, the term *reclaiming* has been used extensively in youth work literature emanating from Israel. More than any other modern nation, Israel has welcomed the world's unwanted children with open arms. First came children from the Holocaust, and in more recent history, children have come from the collapsing Soviet Union, warring nations of Northern Africa, and many other places in the world where the lives of children are considered cheap. These children have found new roots in a nationwide network of youth villages called Youth Aliyah, which means homecoming.

One of the most remarkable examples of reclaiming in the twentieth century is the youth work of Janusz Korczak (1878–1942) of Poland. Trained as a physician, he established an orphanage for Jewish street youth in Warsaw and served as associate director of a similar Christian orphanage. He authored 20 books, including *Children of the Street* (1901), *How to Love a Child* (1929), and *The Child's Right to Respect* (1929).

When German troops invaded Poland, Korczak and his orphans were incarcerated in the Warsaw Ghetto. On August 6, 1942, the troops came to take them away. Accompanied by Korczak and his coworkers, the children were neatly clad in their best clothes as they marched in fours, following the oldest boy who carried a green flag symbolizing life.

Hundreds lined the route to the train station to watch this parade of orphans and the doctor who was one of the most esteemed figures in Warsaw. Fearing a martyr was being created, a high-ranking official approached Korczak to offer him personal asylum. He refused, saying, "Who would abandon children at a time like this?" Although Korczak's life has faded into history, his question still echoes into our times.

Questions for Today

Is reclaiming really possible with today's violent youth? Are there some children who are just beyond hope? Are there issues unique to this generation of young people when compared to those of earlier days? Are there tangible steps that we as caregivers, parents, teachers, clergy, social workers, juvenile justice officials, and concerned citizens can take to help turn the tide of juvenile crime and delinquency?

How do we relate to those kids who distrust and defy adults? With our own children, where is the proper balance between control and independence? How can we raise respectful kids in a disrespectful world? These are but a few of the questions we will grapple with in this book.

Today, many would rather abandon our most troubled and troubling youths. Some youth are like the son in the parable. They come from solid homes, yet have cut themselves off from family, faith, and roots. Others are souls who are starving—spiritual orphans who are growing up unparented, unchurched, and unrooted. For whatever reasons, their "belongings" are broken; yet they are all children of a Father who claims them. These are our modern prodigal sons and daughters, and they are longing to come home, even as they test the limits of our love.

CHAPTER 3

A Rootless Generation
our modern prodigals

Consider these children to have fallen among thieves, the thieves of ignorance and sin and ill fate and loss. Their birthrights were stolen. They have no belongings.
—Karl Menninger, American psychiatrist (1893–1990)

SERIOUS DELINQUENCY AND VIOLENCE were once mainly confined to disadvantaged and blighted urban areas. For most Americans, the victims of youth violence were almost always someone else's children. Not any more. Youth violence has invaded the mainstream of all of our cities, suburbs, and rural communities. One U.S. government study found that one in four modern teens are at risk of failing to successfully cope and achieve productive lives.[1] Where are we going wrong in raising our youth?

Modern families, however they are constituted, are over-stressed and undersupported. Millions of children grow up weakly bonded to parents and enter school undisciplined and primed for conflict. Some schools try to instill obedience with simplistic zero-tolerance policies that rely mainly on punishment and exclusion. Other schools tolerate disruptions and misbehavior, thereby reinforcing delinquent behavior.

Recalcitrant students quickly wear out their welcome and become dropouts and castoffs, expelled to nowhere. Youngsters not bonded to school or to positive peers seek out substitute belongings with other outcast youth. They are then socialized in a youth culture with its own values and norms, which often reject traditional mainstream virtues.

Communities lack the tools to meet the new challenges presented by youth in crisis. Churches are particularly ambivalent about including youth from challenged families, ostensibly because of a desire to protect "good children" from the "bad apple" blight.

When we tried to place a youth from a foster home in a volunteer position at a Bible camp, the director rejected the application, saying, "If he's an at-risk child, I don't want him around here!" Although churches understand that delinquency is a spiritual and moral crisis, faith communities generally have not been on the front lines reaching out to prevent delinquency or to reclaim troubled children.

The first step in solving a problem is to identify clearly what the problem is. Adults often assume they know about adolescence since they were once young themselves. Of course, many of the difficulties faced by today's youth are encountered by every generation. For example, it is common for adults to decry how much worse today's youth are than in their era. In the 1930s, youth were called "the lost generation" by elders with good cause, because millions were homeless and unemployed bums riding the rails during the Depression. But as history shows, that generation of so-called misfits whipped a depression and won a war.

But some problems are unique to our time, for the family has undergone radical changes. In this chapter, we focus our attention on four important challenges facing today's youth. Such problems have always existed, but they arise with greater intensity and peril in what is called the postmodern generation. This is graphically expressed in the following note handed to us by a 15-year-old boy in a detention center:

Please pray for my friend Jared. He hung himself Sunday. I pray that he made it to heaven. Please pray my dad comes home from jail in 30 days and my HIV test comes back with what God wanted it to be.

Whether unique to our time or not, four general characteristics are present in the lives of many of our modern-day prodigals. They are unattached and adult-wary, fatherless in search of an identity, children of rejection and rage, and caught in the web of chemical abuse.

Unattached and Adult-Wary

Psychological Orphans

Children who grow up outside the reach of caring adults are our modern psychological orphans. Delinquency experts once described youth in trouble as being "alienated" from society, which is defined as the "withdrawing or separation of a person's affections from an object or position of former attachment, such as society and family." Many troubled youth today are *beyond* alienation.

Because they have never been attached to society or family, these young people have nothing to be reunited to. They are better described by the term *anomie*, which means "a social instability resulting from an absence of all connectedness, standards, values." The term *anonymous*, from the root word anomie, means "the condition of not being named or identified in any way." While this condition was usually present only in serial killers in years past, many youths today feel this way.

Nicky Cruz, the much-feared New York City gang member from the 1960s, explains these feelings:

I died when I was twelve years old, the day my mother told me I was the son of the devil and she never wanted to see me again. From that moment on, my body was just waiting to catch up with my dead soul. I didn't care about anything or anyone. I didn't care if I lived or died.[2]

That is what made Nicky so dangerous.

Because of this anomic condition, the concept of rehabilitation has become somewhat outdated as well. *Rehabilitation* means "to restore to a former state." But what state does a *rootless* youth have to be rehabilitated to? That life needs to be reformed, and that generally happens only in the context of a long-term relationship with a committed, caring adult who makes a place for such a youth to belong.

When angry and adult-wary youth display antisocial behavior, communities respond to this threat with calls to restore discipline. This seems sensible because many youths certainly are not self-disciplined. The word *discipline* comes from the word *disciple*, and that is precisely the point: many youths have no positive role models in their lives. They are "discipled" by other troubled teens. Calls to "get tough" only address the symptoms and lead to simplistic "fight or flight" reactions that seek to attack or banish our problem youth. But it is contradictory to think we can reclaim antisocial youth by expelling them from the social bond.

A child's most basic psychological need is for love—to find a secure bond with at least one other human. When the love of a caregiver is threatened, initially the child tries to find affection. This is typically accomplished by attempting to please the parent, by crying, or by otherwise trying to gain sympathy. If affection is not received, youth may seek it elsewhere in substitute relationships. A 13-year-old boy who shot several peers outside his school was known by his church youth group leader as a perfect child. He stood out from peers because of his willingness to do anything to please adults. What seemed like a sign of respect and generosity on the surface was probably signaling his starvation for love.

When attempts to find affection fail, youngsters become frustrated and angry, and the child who feels rejected often rages at adults. Hostility is a hollow substitute for love, but at least such interaction prevents a child from being ignored. As one young man in jail poignantly told us, "I'd rather be wanted for some crime than not wanted at all."

If this strategy is futile, the next step is to give up on relationships altogether. It is typical for a child at this stage to become angry and depressed, then to withdraw from or actively shun adults. Such behavior reflects the inhibition of the natural hunger for human attachment to avoid the pain of further rejection.

Fortunately, in most cases where youth are ignored or rejected by caregivers, they find substitute relationships of belonging, perhaps with a relative, teacher, neighbor, or with siblings or peers. But if no substitute attachments are found, the child may rage or become increasingly empty and devoid of affection. Because the need for attachment is so basic to survival, psychiatrists like Lauretta Bender conclude that such children are not *completely* affectionless. Rather, they should be considered *relatively* affectionless. Most children who do not show affection still have the potential to form meaningful relationships, but because they are shutting others out to avoid being hurt again, it takes time for anyone to win their trust.

The Careless Conscience

Children deprived of caring become children who do not care. The most damaging effect of attachment problems is the failure of the conscience to develop properly. At the end of the nineteenth century, psychologists and criminologists began studying persons whose consciences were retarded. They were called *moral imbeciles*, for delinquency was thought to be a genetic disorder inherited from criminal parents. Later evidence suggested that conscience problems result more from lack of nurture than from nature.

Over the course of the twentieth century, these children were called *asocial, psychopathic, sociopathic, affectionless,* and even *predators*—all labels that are more pejorative than scientific. More recently, common psychiatric diagnoses are *attachment disorder, conduct disorder, oppositional defiant disorder,* or *disruptive behavior disorder.* Perhaps the most simple and profound label applied to this problem is the one coined by psychiatrist

David Levy. In 1937, he wrote that children who appear to have no conscience suffer from "affect hunger."[3]

The earliest scientific research on conscience focused on children who lived in cold, custodial orphanages in the early twentieth century. These infants and children were locked away, deprived of social interaction, and merely clothed, fed, and warehoused. Many died under these conditions, and those who survived grew up to be affectionless, devoid of guilt, and seemingly unable to learn from experience.

Such sterile orphanages are now closed, but we are still raising generations of children who are poorly bonded to adults and who do not adopt moral values. How does this happen? When social bonds between adult and child are absent, children have no reason to want to please adults. Why? Because the most powerful restraints on disrespectful behavior have always been healthy human attachments.

In the popular press it has been common to label seriously delinquent children as sociopaths who have no feelings for others and who are devoid of conscience. These labels are even used by a few professionals who make a diagnosis based on an office interview or second-hand accounts of violent behavior. However, prominent experts who have carefully studied these youth caution against jumping to the conclusion that any child who is still in the developmental process lacks a conscience.

Fritz Redl, author of the classic book, *Children Who Hate*, worked for 50 years with delinquents in both Austria and the United States. In a demonstration project at the National Institute of Mental Health, Redl searched 200 children's psychiatric hospitals to find the most aggressive boys in the country. After exhaustive work with them in a residential setting, he concluded that delinquent thinking often distorted the conscience, but that if adults look closely, they will find some positives in every child.

Some high-risk young people, like the one in the following story, have what Redl called a "Swiss cheese" conscience. They operate mostly on the "might makes right" or "honor among thieves" principles of moral development.

Did Yummy Have a Conscience?

Not many mourned the death of neighborhood bully Yummy Sandifer. On a mission for older gang members whom he idolized, 11-year-old Yummy shot and killed a 14-year-old girl who was in the wrong place at the wrong time. To avoid apprehension by the police, other involved gang members murdered Yummy in return. Yummy's mother had been arrested 41 times, mostly for prostitution. Her little boy was not far behind with his own felony count of 23.

Pursued by police and peers, Yummy was last seen on a neighbor's porch, asking the woman if they could pray together. He wanted her to call his grandmother so he could turn himself in. Before she could return, Yummy was gone. He was later found murdered.

A Cook County official declared, "If ever there was a case where the kid's future was predictable, it was this case . . . here was a kid who was made and turned into a sociopath by the time he was 3 years old."

The fat case files of failed interventions with kids like Yummy certainly would suggest they may be hopeless. But these reports are produced by office-based professionals who are rarely allowed entrance into the world of an adult-wary kid. We see quite another side of Yummy when we listen to a friend who was interviewed by *Time* magazine:

> "Everyone thinks he was a bad person, but he respected my mom, who's got cancer," says twelve-year-old Kenyata Jones. He and Yummy used to regularly have sleep-overs where they would bake cookies and brownies and rent movies like *The Little Rascals*.
>
> "He was my friend, you know. I just cried and cried at school when I heard about what happened. And I'm gonna cry some more today, and I'm gonna cry some more tomorrow, too."[4]

Youth like Yummy certainly need intense help in changing their thinking errors and rebuilding their weak consciences. Such youth who are cut off from adults or positive peers are at risk of developing lifelong antisocial personalities.

But we should not assume that a person with a weak conscience can never advance to higher levels of conscience. Conversions are possible, and young people in particular are developmentally very malleable. We have seen many youth who seemed totally unable to attach to adults. But with proper nurturing, limits, and greater maturity, they were able to turn their lives around.

Fatherless in Search of an Identity

Children with absent, uninvolved, or abusive fathers are profoundly overrepresented in delinquency and school disruption statistics. As early as the 1960s, a study commissioned by President Richard Nixon and headed by Senator Daniel Patrick Moynihan predicted that massive social disorganization would ensue when fatherless children exceeded the statistical breakpoint of 27%.[5] By the close of the millennium, the rate of fatherlessness had exceeded 50% in many racial minority groups. Among whites, fatherlessness had affected one in five children, representing a tenfold increase within one generation.[6]

While many single mothers are closely bonded to their children, both boys and girls are at a greater risk of delinquency in the absence of caring male role models. When girls hunger for male attachments, they may become prematurely sexually active. Both boys and girls benefit from a caring male model to develop positive sexual values and identity. The sexually promiscuous behavior of delinquents often springs from the almost total absence of caring males in the home or school experience.

Dr. David Popenoe, professor of sociology at Rutgers University, explains the problem in this way:

> Teenage boys without fathers are notoriously prone to trouble. The pathway to adulthood for daughters is some-

what easier, but they still must learn from their fathers, as they cannot from their mothers, how to relate to men. They learn from their fathers about heterosexual trust, intimacy, and [the] difference [between the sexes]. They learn to appreciate their own femininity from the one male who is most special in their lives. . . . Most importantly, through loving and being loved by their fathers, they learn that they are love-worthy.7

A committee assembled by the National Research Council's Board on Children and Families examined the effects of fathers playing with their children and how that relates to the emotional well-being of the children. The study concluded that at play and in other realms, fathers tend to stress challenge, initiative, risk-taking, and independence. Mothers, on the other hand, focus on the equally important qualities of emotional security and personal safety.8 On the playground, for example, fathers may try to get their child to swing higher than the child on the next swing. With the child's arms flailing and the child gasping for air, the father appears to be having much more fun than his child. Mothers tend to play much differently with their children. They are inclined to be more protective, worrying more about the possibility of an accident.

It is this male type of playing—pushing children beyond their comfort zone—that helps teach children confidence in trying new things. Both types of playing are essential for children. But without a male playing with them (a relative, day-care worker, or baby sitter), they miss out on an important developmental influence. In fact, one study of convicted murderers in Texas found that 90% of them either did not play with their father as children, or played abnormally.9

Father-son play can also help promote the essential virtue of self-control. According to psychologist John Snarey, children who roughhouse with their fathers usually learn quickly that biting, kicking, and other forms of physical violence are not acceptable.10 They learn about personal restraint, a trait virtually absent in most troubled youth.

Does the lack of positive male influence eliminate hope for those beyond their formative years? No. But it does require that someone assume the role of a father, particularly for boys who have never had one.

Why is that so important? Writer and social commentator Robert Bly illustrates one answer in this way:

> When a father and son spend long hours together we could say that a substance almost like food passes from the older body to the younger. The son's body—not his mind—receives, and the father gives this food at a level far below consciousness. His cells receive some knowledge of what an adult masculine body is. The younger body learns at what frequency the masculine body vibrates. It begins to grasp the song that adult male cells sing.[11]

While a mother does many essential things, one thing she cannot do is to model for a boy how to be a man. In a *Los Angeles Times Magazine* cover story, "Mothers, Sons, and the Gangs," each of the several single mothers interviewed lamented, "I don't understand why my boy hangs out on the streets. I'm a good mother. I keep a clean house. I go to church. I don't run around with men. I cook for the boy, wash his clothes, and provide a good home. Why doesn't he want to stay here?"[12]

We have noticed that when our male college students begin elementary school internships, they are literally deluged by father-hungry children who cling to them. These children know what they need; they have found a rare missing treasure.

While many troubled teens take on an angry demeanor whenever the topic of fathers comes up, their feelings are not always consistent. Straight Ahead staff member Peter Vanacore recalls being at a campfire with a group of inner-city boys toward the end of a 10-day wilderness trip. He asked them to tell about their fathers.

The first boy to speak angrily spewed, "I hate my father!" Peter became concerned as the mood became considerably more hostile with each boy who spoke.

Just as he was about to try to defuse the potentially explosive mood, the last boy spoke up. "You know, I really love my father. I've never met him. But I really love him." One by one, each of the boys told similar stories of how they, too, loved their fathers.

This anecdote reveals just how important fathers are, and how conflicted our views of our fathers can be. It also illustrates why we must never speak ill of any child's parents while in his or her presence, no matter how poor a job of parenting we might think they have done.

The Power of Mothers

Does the need for a father negate the importance of a mother figure? Not at all. We have also worked with many boys who had been abandoned by their mothers, sometimes as infants. There is no doubt that they were among the most damaged and maladjusted of all the children in our programs. Fortunately, far fewer children suffer the ill effects from a mother's neglect than from a father's.

One Child, Two Hands

One of the great art treasures of the world is *The Return of the Prodigal Son,* a painting by Rembrandt that is housed in the Hermitage in St. Petersburg, Russia.

A son in tattered clothing kneels at the feet of a father who embraces him with both hands. Upon closer inspection of the painting, we can see that Rembrandt painted one hand as the hand of the father and the other hand as the hand of the mother.

The hand of the father is one of strength, supporting the son. The mother's hand is one of gentleness, consoling and nurturing the boy. Raising children is a two-handed job that requires both strength and gentleness.

We conducted a group activity where we asked youth to name their biggest heroes. While one might expect to hear the names of professional athletes or musicians, almost without exception, the youth say either "my mother" or "my grandmother."

While it is difficult to describe God as a heavenly Father to many youths, at the same time it allows us to effectively use the illustration of a mother image. For example, we were recently struggling to explain to a group of boys in jail what God is like. We explained, "God is a father who thinks about you continuously, who loves you no matter what you've done, who wants nothing more than to just be with you—" As we were searching for the next descriptive phrase, one of the boys finished the sentence: "—who's just like your mother." All the boys nodded with understanding.

The Bible makes it clear that God is not only masculine. In fact, one of the Hebrew names for God, *El Shaddai,* comes from the noun *Shad,* which is literally translated as *breast.* The most tender title used of God, the name *El Shaddai,* describes God's more nurturing motherly attribute of supplying sustenance, strength, satisfaction, and sufficiency. This is beautifully illustrated in Isaiah 66:13: "As a mother comforts her child, so will I comfort you."

Children of Rejection and Rage

Children who act in mean and cruel ways are seething in anger, possessing what psychologist Louis Ramey termed "free-floating anger." This anger is accompanied with feelings of frustration and helplessness, which make them perpetually irritable like a person who wakes up on the wrong side of the bed day after day.[13]

When we ask youths in detention to estimate the level of their anger on a thermometer from 0 to 10, most say that they never get below 7 or 8 even in the best of times. As they carry their fury around, strapped on like short-fused dynamite, they are a danger zone waiting to be ignited. A slight provocation, such as being disrespected on the street by a peer or being corrected by a teacher in school, triggers an explosion. This kind of deep-seated anger is defined as *rage*. Where does it come from? Often it comes from experiencing rejection at an early age from close family members.

In one detention center we asked a group of young people, "How many of you experienced rejection while growing up?" Out of 12 in the group, 5 told stories of how a father or stepfather had tried to kill or seriously hurt them when they were young. It is not surprising that when on the streets, these young men are a terror to the community.

Don't Take It Personally

One night several boys tried to escape from a detention center where Scott and Hanne Larson lead a Bible study. Fortunately, nobody was hurt. All were caught and locked in their rooms for the next three weeks. Food was brought in to them, and they were only allowed out to go to the bathroom and to shower. All furniture was removed, and rooms were bare except for a mattress on the floor.

José, a boy who had been attending the Bible study, was one of those locked in his room. During the third week of isolation, he cracked and asked a staff member if Scott could come in and visit him.

Scott recalls their meeting:

When I entered his room, I wasn't prepared for what I saw. José was standing in the corner of the room with his back against the wall and repeatedly banging the wall with the back of his head and clenched hand. He was so absorbed by his anger that he could not even focus on the fact that I was in the room.

I watched him for a little while, not really knowing what to say or do. Then gently, I put my arm around him. As I began to pull him toward me, José started hitting my chest instead of the wall. He was not trying to hurt me; he just needed an outlet for his anger and frustration.

I kept my arms around him until eventually his blows became softer and softer. Then José started to cry, and for the first time we actually made eye contact.

"I just need you to pray for me," he sobbed. "I've blown it so bad. I've let everyone down. My family, the staff, you, God. Everybody."

I suggested that he just say those same things to God directly. He did, and it was one of the most beautiful prayers I had ever heard. I'm sure this was the first time in three weeks that José felt at peace.

The Bible teaches about love's power to constrain.[14] Though not a word often used today, constraint actually means "to hold together, to keep in, to be taken up with." How opposite this is from restraint, the approach most commonly applied to teens who get out of control. Restraint means "to deprive of liberty, to hold back, to limit." Restraint will never lower the anger level in a child. It cannot touch his or her need for acceptance and unconditional love. Yet when someone feels unconditionally loved, even at their worst, slowly the anger thermometer can begin to cool down. From 7 to 6. From 6 to 4.

Less easily identified than the José's of the world are those victimized and bullied children who ruminate in bitter silence until one day a weapon provides them with the power to explode in revenge. At the most socialized extreme are passive-aggressive children. Nicholas Long calls them "Kids with angry smiles." While they never seriously violate any law, they act out their antagonism in ways that infuriate the adults in their lives.

In any case, children filled with anger are very difficult to work with. Their anger tends to bring out our anger. It takes a remarkable person, with a great deal of insight and personal sense of security, to effectively deal with such a child.

Hanne Larson's first work with youth was with girls in the housing projects of Minneapolis. They would often say things like "I hate you and never want to see you again!" When asked why she kept working with such "ungrateful little brats," she would say, "Their anger isn't directed at me. Sometimes I'm just a safe place for them to vent it." Somehow she was able (most of the time) not to take it personally when teenage girls who were hurting unloaded their rage onto her.

Over time, the anger in many of them began to lose its strength as they experienced a person who knew them at their worst, yet still loved them. Although Hanne has not lived in Minnesota for many years, she still receives calls and letters from many of those girls whose lives have forever been affected by her love and acceptance.

One such phone call came from Tina, who said,

> I just wanted you to know how often I think about you, Hanne. I have three kids of my own now. I want to raise them the way God wants me to, but most of the time I feel at a loss when it comes to knowing what He would want me to do. That's when I think of you. I ask myself, "What would Hanne do?" and then I know that's probably what God would want.

Caught in the Web of Chemical Abuse

No doubt children use drugs and alcohol for many of the same reasons as their elders did a generation earlier—to satisfy their curiosity, to lubricate social relationships, to escape from pain, to protest and rebel. Yet one of the biggest differences between youth today and those from generations past is the degree of hurt and pain that they carry. While children use all kinds of different drugs, marijuana has been by far the most popular. Why? As one boy explains, "It's Novocaine for the soul." We have heard numerous young people state, "I can give up crime. I can give up alcohol. I can even give up sex. But I can't give up herb."

Not only do our most disadvantaged youth turn to drugs, however. One middle-class couple told us of their struggles with their son:

"Jimmy had always been a straight-A student. He loved sports. He loved life. But now, in his senior year, everything has changed. Marijuana—and who knows what else—has taken over his life. We've tried to talk about it. We've tried grounding him. We've threatened to put him into a drug program. He only seems to be getting worse. At this point, he'll be lucky if he graduates. Whatever it takes, we're willing to do it. Somebody just tell us. We can't go on like this; it's destroying our whole family."

It is helpful to hear what teens say about this problem. The youth in the feature on the next page are participants in a program for youth with alcohol and behavioral problems.[15]

Jamie C. Chambers, a professor at North American Baptist Seminary and a specialist on youth substance abuse, makes a distinction between friendships and "drugships." While friendships place priority on people over things and achievements, drugships are relationships centered around drug use. Chambers describes a passion that kids can develop with chemicals, where an almost romance-like bond develops between the youngster and his or her drug of choice.[16]

Of course, this does not happen overnight. The spell cast by chemicals is gradual. Addiction experts such as Tammy Bell describe the process as one that happens in four distinct stages:

1. Experimenting. Children typically begin at the first stage of experimenting with chemical use. This is generally motivated by their desire for either pleasure or escape.

2. Psychosocial dependence. At this point, children use chemicals to help them accomplish things they do not believe they could do without them, such as asking someone out on a date. When a young person begins bonding with drugs or alcohol to accomplish things in several areas of life, they are well on their way to addiction.

Teens Describe Substance Abuse

Jason: I'd come home from partying and mom would ask like where were you and start yelling at me and I'd say it's none of your business anyway. I'd start yelling at her and swearing back at her. In school, [when] teachers would say something, I'd yell at them back, get kicked out of the classroom, [I'd] start getting into fights, punching and swearing.

Daisy: I always wanted to be a nurse like my mom. When I started drinking, I remember saying I was going to move in with my friends. I was going to quit school and be a waitress or something just to make enough money so I could go out and drink again. Before, I wanted to graduate from high school and go on to college.

Kristi: When I was high, I was really paranoid. I always thought they're going to find out, I'd better get rid of them. I got rid of my family, threw away school, track, my job, trust with everybody in the community, religion, everything.

Jerry: I think it helps the most just to be able to talk to people your own age that are going through the same stuff and you can connect with them. Somebody older telling youth what to do, you just block him out. You don't want to listen to them because they're older and they think they have power over you.

Amy: AA has helped to break down my denial system by teaching me to tell people what's upsetting me rather than saying nothing's wrong. It's taught me to be more honest with myself and family. I've hurt them and hurt myself by stealing or running away or putting myself into bad situations with guys.

Sarah: My group has helped me by teaching me that it's okay to talk about frustration. It has taught me about forgiveness. Meaning, I need to forgive myself before I can honestly forgive others.

—These students are from Woodland Hills, a Positive Peer Culture treatment program in Duluth, Minnesota.

3. Harmful use. Here adolescents become so involved with chemicals that they depend on them just to cope and maintain stability. They often develop an increasing tolerance to the chemical and require increased dosage to achieve the same high. Not only is their consumption increasing, the negative consequences of their decisions are escalating as well. At this point, however, they still do not experience withdrawal when they stop using the chemical.

4. Core addiction. One of the differences between harmful acts and the final stage of core addiction lies in the presence of withdrawal symptoms. With full-blown addiction, withdrawal symptoms accompany any attempt to stop consumption. Core addiction probably has a genetic basis, which heightens the risk of relapse.

Young people who become chemically involved have also mastered the art of denial along the way. They tend to deny the fact of their using, the impact of their using, and the reality of their inability to make good choices. Without outside intervention, the road for these young people is one of disaster. While treatment can be very painful, involved, and complex, addictions are overcome only when youth have solid, long-term relationships with persons who are willing to walk with them through the storm.

One of the most important challenges we face as adults is to understand and counteract the hazardous environments that are so detrimentally influencing our youth. This is the focus of the next chapter.

CHAPTER 4

The Broken Community

relationships at risk

> *Where neglect once finds a foothold, other injustices multiply.*
> —Dorothea Dix, American mental health pioneer
> (1802–1887)

THE PROBLEMS OF CHILDREN cannot be understood in isolation from the environments where they are raised. Prominent psychologist Urie Bronfenbrenner defines what he calls "the ecology of childhood" as consisting of family, school, peers, and the broader community, which includes neighborhoods and religious and social institutions. In the following discussion, we consider these "environmental hazards" and suggest promising solutions for rebuilding our broken communities. The following chart lists the four key relationships in a youth's life. In the pages to follow, we will address what happens when these relationships malfunction:

HEALTHY RELATIONSHIPS	RELATIONSHIPS AT RISK
1. Bonded Securely to Family	1. Families on the Edge
2. Bonded to School	2. Estranged From School
3. Bonded to Prosocial Peers	3. Destructive Peer Influence
4. Bonded to Community	4. Children of Exile

Families on the Edge

Wayward children are not created in a vacuum. Each is influenced by myriad forces—family, schools, peers, neighborhoods, social institutions, and churches. Without a doubt, the most potent of all influences in the life of the child is the family. And so, when a child exhibits a problem, many are quick to blame it on the family. But parents of troubled children do not need blame. Barbara Huff of the Federation of Families for Children's Mental Health calls for a moratorium on the adjective "dysfunctional" when describing families. If labels are needed, better terms might be "overstressed" or "undersupported."

Many resilient children from highly stressed families somehow turn out all right, while other children who are reared in warm, nurturing, and supportive environments can end up in deep trouble. Sometimes one child in a family does well and another falters. At other times, the temperament of a child or some underlying disability further complicates the parenting process. All in all, there are no "quick and easy formulas" to produce healthy children, but there are a few key principles.

Normally, stable families provide the nurturing bonds and corrective guidance that children need. However, when families become stressed, they are often not able to fully meet the needs of children. Ironically, the struggles of adolescent children often produce much of that stress. Even the most solid family can develop serious problems when it becomes overwhelmed by stress and conflict, as illustrated in the example of Carrie and her parents.

"Where did we go wrong?"

Carrie had always been her mother's pride and joy and the apple of her father's eye. But when she turned 14, nothing they did seemed to work anymore. Her parents had been suspicious for some time, but a police call confirmed their worst nightmares.

Carrie had told her parents she was staying overnight at a friend's house, where she and Sara would be watching videos all night. Yet the police were giving an entirely different story. Neighbors had complained of loud music just after 11 o'clock. An investigation revealed that 26 freshmen classmates were having a party while Sara's parents were gone for the weekend. Sara had been left in the care of her older sister, who was spending the evening with her boyfriend.

"There were several bottles of hard liquor and numerous drugs confiscated tonight," reported the investigating officer. "Your daughter Carrie is in the bathroom vomiting. She's had a lot to drink. You better come down to the station right away." A million questions raced through Nancy and Michael's heads as they headed out the door. How had this happened? Where were Sara's parents? How could Carrie have lied to us like this? Who knows what else was going on over there? What if she is pregnant, too? Anger was seething from both of them by the time they reached the station.

In the aftermath, the conflict began to shift from Carrie to her parents. "If you hadn't been so selfish, wanting the prestige of a vice presidency in your company, this never would have happened," blamed Nancy. "You never once considered us in your decision to uproot and move us a thousand miles across the country. Did it ever occur to you that maybe this was a sacrifice not worth making?! Back in Youngstown, Carrie had good friends, loved the church youth group, and would never have been involved in something like this! I hope your new position has been worth it!"

Michael was equally infuriated. He had worked long and hard to provide the extra things he was now able to give his family. He had not heard Nancy complain the day they moved out of their cramped three-bedroom rambler in Ohio into a spacious four-bedroom colonial in a prestigious development of a wealthy suburb. He did not like the extra hours he worked either, but he was doing it for his family. He was sure this would not have happened if Nancy had worked harder to find a church with a good youth group instead of spending all of her time buying new things for the house.

Meanwhile, the incident was reported in the local newspaper and was the talk of the town. The youth who were at the party were not only suspended from school, but were also kicked out of extracurricular activities. So far, the only positive thing Carrie had taken up since the move to Massachusetts was soccer, and now she was out of that too. Michael and Nancy felt extremely embarrassed, isolated, and angry.

Family therapists Jack and Judith Balswick note how the parenting of adolescents often occurs during two developmental stresses. The first is the difficult transition period into adolescence. As if that were not enough, parents are often entering their own stressful stage of midlife as well. Adolescent stress does not merely add to parental midlife stress, it multiplies it. The effects of the parents' midlife stress also multiplies the stress experienced by the adolescent. The two must be seen as interactive. Whenever more than one family member is experiencing great personal anxiety, the potential for conflict in the family increases exponentially.[1] As was the case with Carrie's parents, career changes, the stresses of relocating, and the feelings of failure, isolation, and inadequacy can all cause couples to become polarized, rather than being able to draw strength from one another.

Collaboration between parents and professionals is also crucial, because parents are the child's first and most powerful teachers. But parents of troubled youth are often blamed for the problems of their children. Both the public and the professionals who work with youth tend to have negative stereotypes about parents of troubled youth, assuming that they are disinterested and incompetent. Teachers and other youth professionals often list parent contact as a major factor in their job dissatisfaction. Many are intimidated by parents and seek to avoid them, or if they are forced to interact with parents, they do so as adversaries. In turn, parents often feel put down by professionals and also respond with avoidance and anger.

While parents of other special-needs children, such as those with learning disabilities or mental retardation, support one another in formal and informal associations, families of troubled children have been the last to organize. This is changing, though, as organizations like the Federation of Families for Children's Mental Health provide advocacy for families. Among the many positive benefits of such parent associations is their role in advocating for appropriate services for their troubled children.

Estranged From School

A successful school experience is a prerequisite for survival in modern society. Schools deliver not only academic and vocational competence, but they have historically supported the family in fostering moral development. Traditionally, children who did not receive discipline at home could receive it at school. From the 1840s until the 1920s, the *McGuffey Readers* were a common text in American schools. These books were full of lessons for building a student's moral virtues and sense of civic responsibility.

Unfortunately, many modern schools have become large, depersonalized factories that dispense a narrow academic curriculum. As a result, they are ill-equipped to build the character that children need. Linda Lantieri, founder of the Resolving Conflict Creatively Program, contends that today's schools are educating the head but neglecting the heart.[2]

Children in conflict at schools are also at high risk for being excluded, dropping out, and becoming delinquent. In some cases, their anger erupts into rage and violence of frightening proportions. Angry and disturbed youth carry their problems to schools, which then become staging areas for attacks against authority or peers. One girl described it this way: "I wanted to cause others as much pain as I felt. My hurt was getting totally out of control." Understandably, overwhelmed educators begin to treat problem students as lost causes rather than as lost prizes.

When They Stopped Paying Attention

Brian was raised by an alcoholic, single mother. From an early age he grew accustomed to getting himself ready for school. He would often arrive home only to find his mother in a drunken state. After sobering up, she would feel guilty and often say, "You don't have to go to school today, Bry. Let's just the two of us go shopping."

But Brian liked school. It was the only place where people gave him positive attention. But it certainly was not easy for him. In addition to his other problems, in the first grade, Brian had been diagnosed with attention deficit disorder and a moderate speech impediment. So what kept him going to school despite the lack of support at home? Brian answers in his own words:

> It seemed like every year I always had at least one teacher who complimented me on my work. It was because of them that I kept going and doing my homework. Then about the time I was losing interest in school, I started middle school. There the principal took a real interest in me. He knew my mom and my situation, and he would keep tabs on me. Any time I would skip school he'd call me into his office and talk with me, just like a dad. I credit him with the reason I graduated from middle school with honors!

But when Brian moved into the larger high school, he did not have anyone to take the interest in him that his former principal had. Without that connection, Brian began skipping school. Suspensions soon followed.

Before long, he was spending most of his time with older peers who were part of a local gang. By age 14, he found himself at the scene of a teenage gang brawl in which one youngster died. Brian spent the next several years in an institution for delinquents.

But there, a caring, positive teacher began encouraging him and rekindling his interest in academics. After his release, Brian chose to move into a home operated by Straight Ahead Ministries, where he finished high school and went on to a liberal arts college. After graduating with high honors in philosophy and theology, Brian scored in the 95th percentile of his law school entrance exams and was admitted on a full scholarship.

Education and Values

Traditional education is practiced the world over, even in the absence of formal schools for learning. Many tribal cultures are much more child-oriented than Western society. The following chart examines how these traditional values differ from those practiced in highly bureaucratic schools:

TRADITIONAL CONCEPTS OF EDUCATION VERSUS BUREAUCRATIC CONCEPTS OF EDUCATION	
1. Learning occurs in a caring community	1. Schools are large and depersonalized
2. Children are seen as spiritual beings	2. Spirituality is kept out of schools
3. Family is the fountain of learning	3. Education is a job for professionals
4. Elders have important roles	4. Only certified personnel teach
5. Cross-age peer learning is encouraged	5. Students are rigidly segregated by age
6. Hands-on "brain-friendly" learning occurs	6. Brain-antagonistic "seatwork" is preferred
7. Teaching is done with stories and ceremonies	7. Teachers follow the approved curriculum
8. Competition is with peers	8. Competition is against peers
9. Motivation is task-oriented: "do your best"	9. Motivation is ego-oriented: "be the best"
10. Learning is to better serve others	10. Learning is to gain an advantage over others

This chart suggests why Western concepts of education have not well served students from traditional tribal cultures, such as Native Americans, African Americans, and Aboriginal peoples throughout the world. Parents who want a stronger spiritual component to learning also have criticized the bureaucratic school. When we presented this list to a class of parents, one mother said that these were the main reasons she chose to home-school her children. Fortunately, many public and private schools are breaking away from stultifying traditions and creating brain-friendly, family-friendly, value-friendly learning environments.

Sometimes school authorities work valiantly to keep kids connected to school. But if the youth is seen as a troublemaker, he or she may subtly or directly be encouraged to leave. When we met with youth in a Vermont school, one girl spoke of how certain teachers quit talking to her after she became pregnant.

Another boy recalled his first meeting with a teacher at the beginning of the school year. Because he had experienced problems with that teacher the previous spring, he decided to get off to a good start with a smile and a greeting when he met the teacher in the halls. The teacher's icy response was, "Are you still here? I thought you would have dropped out by now." Though such disrespect is rare, it takes only one unprofessional teacher to spell disaster for a student on the edge.

The reality is that most kids who formally drop out were not bonded to school in the first place. One study found that only one out of seven students who drop out have ever even discussed their plans with a teacher. Phi Delta Kappa researchers suggest that schools stop quoting *dropout percentages,* which imply that these students do not measure up to standards. Instead, perhaps schools should measure their own performance by publicizing *school holding power percentages.*[3] After all, who would fly with an airline advertising that 75% of its passengers arrive safely at their destinations?

Children who drop out of school are not necessarily any less intelligent or less motivated than those who finish high school. Rather, many of them just learn in a style that is not compatible with the typical educational system. When we present the information in ways that they can best receive it, many potential dropouts remain motivated to learn and graduate.

Educational Disability

Independent of all other risk factors, failure in school is one of the most powerful predictors of delinquency. Prisons are full of school dropouts and "pushouts" whose trajectory to crime started with school failure. We also know that a majority of youth who become chronic delinquents have emotional disturbances and learning disabilities that interfere with school success. Many have not received special education services to which they are entitled.

Some behavior and learning disabilities are related to variations in brain functioning. For example, the effects of fetal alcohol or drug poisoning handicap many children. Sometimes these children are slow in learning academic and social skills and retarded in conscience development. Children with attention deficit hyperactive disorders (ADHD) are at very high risk of delinquency. Even if disabilities are brain-based, proper special education can often avert school failure and thus reduce the risk of delinquency.

Many cases of ADHD are caused by lead poisoning. The United States has the highest rate of ADHD in the world, although some cases can be prevented by removing the toxic lead still contaminating inner-city tenements. We also can easily identify children suffering from lead poisoning and offer intensive remedial education as needed.

Decades of studies from the University of Pittsburgh Medical School suggest that among African American children, lead poisoning is also a significant cause of academic retardation and behavioral disorders. But exposure to lead is not just a problem that affects poor children. Studies show that as many as 9% of the children in middle-class urban neighborhoods have toxic levels of lead.[4]

Parent advocacy groups such as PACER (Parent Advocacy Coalition for Educational Rights) have been among the leaders in the movement to provide appropriate special education services to children with emotional and behavior disabilities. These students are more likely to drop out of school than are mentally retarded students. A large number of youth in the juvenile system need special education services to develop skills needed to compete in an information society.[5]

Destructive Peer Influence

Peer influence becomes potent as soon as a child enters school. Typically, a youngster becomes steadily more responsive to children his or her age and less dependent on adults as he or she moves toward adolescence. Positive relationships between child and parent can buffer the youth from excessive negative influence by peers.

While parents cannot completely control who their child chooses as friends, in most cases, young people gravitate to peers who do not pose a major threat to their values. Contrary to popular thinking, most teens remain strongly bonded to their family, have values similar to their parents, and turn to their parents in times of stress.

But when adults are not a prominent force in the lives of children and youth, then the peer culture, the gang, the cult, and the culture of the street can gain a powerful hold over children's lives. Children who lack positive relationships to adults usually seek peers with similar problems. Even children from good families can sometimes be drawn into deep troubles by their peer associations. While peers can be a force for good, negative groups can foster delinquent thinking and values, anesthetizing the conscience and leading to destructive behavior.

Antisocial youth gangs in any culture are caused by a great gulf between youth and elders. Youth who are weakly bonded to parents—or who gain premature independence—form their own youth culture, complete with alternative values, heroes, myths, and artifacts.

A Worldwide Youth Culture

As we have traveled on many continents, we have been amazed that youth everywhere appear more like one another than like their own elders. American styles of clothing, music, and entertainment have become icons to youth worldwide. Children in tribal villages proudly display T-shirts with English-language slogans they cannot read. One of the principal youth gangs in South Africa calls itself "The Americans." Youths in a Capetown institution performed for us the latest rock music that is alien to adults everywhere on earth but familiar to all of their children.

No longer only representative of a violent urban subculture, popular clothing styles now originate more from the street gangs of Los Angeles, Chicago, and New York City than from Calvin Klein designers. In fact, some designers of sneakers even do market testing among young New York City offenders before manufacturing and mass-marketing products to the larger youth market. As gangster styles of dress become mainstream and sexually exploitative, and drug culture lyrics abound, it seems that the most value-depleted messages of the youth culture are being elevated by media and advertisers to the status of fashion.

Carl Taylor, a professor at Michigan State University and a gang violence researcher, told us of a recent to trip to Germany where he was working with fringe youth. In his discussion with one very apathetic young man, Taylor asked him what one thing he really cared about. To this, the blonde-haired youth responded, "Tupak." When hip-hop rapper Tupak Shakur was murdered in 1997, he became immortalized just as Elvis was to earlier generations. Many youth emphatically insist that Tupak is still alive, just as some believe Elvis still lives, years after his death.

In underdeveloped countries we find entire cultures of street children, not bonded to any adults and living by their own code. Jack Kirkland, an international expert on youth, predicts that America soon will see large numbers of these street children in every major city.[6]

Gangs as Substitute Families

Gangs meet the most basic human needs for children who have been cast out of mainstream society. One teen told us:

> The gang gave me something I felt I could be part of. For the first time in my life I had a goal—something I could strive for. I wanted to climb up to a position in the gang where I would be recognized and given respect by everyone. And I would do whatever it took to get that.
>
> That gang quickly became my family. I spent all my time with them: making more money, going to parties, and hanging out with girls, drinking and getting high. That's what I thought life was about—doing all those stupid things.
>
> I remember one of the leaders who became like a father to me, although he was only 18. He was both highly respected and feared in the neighborhood. I would go to him for advice a lot, and he was the one who got me my first gun.

Though gangs are largely seen as a modern-day phenomenon, Frederic Thrasher, in his 1927 sociological classic, *The Gang*, identified more than 1,300 Chicago gangs. He concluded that youth *need* gangs, and that for adolescents aged 11 to 17, an elemental desire for gang membership is usually present.[7] The only question was: What kind of gang would they join?

In his 1923 book, *The Unadjusted Girl: A Study of Prostitutes, Runaways, and Maladjusted Girls*, William Thomas found that unadjusted girls were unable to adequately satisfy their basic desires for adventure, security, love, and recognition.[8] Young people not getting their needs met in one or more of these areas are much more likely to join destructive gangs in an attempt to satisfy needs.

Can gangs ever be good? Yes. In many ways, groups such as Girl Scouts, sports teams, music groups, drama clubs, and faith communities can be like gangs. Perhaps one of the best examples was the first-century church. All four basic desires were abundantly met there. Adventure and living on the edge were commonplace, and there was a clear sense of purpose and one-ness, of being a part of something big and powerful. Church members were also known for their love for each other and for recognizing individual talents. And what camaraderie! This unity, as well as their strong faith, made them feel secure:

> All who believed were together and had all things in common. They would sell their possessions and goods and distribute the proceeds to all, as any had need. Day by day, as they spent much time together in the temple, they broke bread at home and ate their food with glad and generous hearts.[9]

The Greek word describing this sort of fellowship is *koinonea*, which literally means "to give, contribute, share; to be initiated into the mysteries; to participate in the deeds of others, being equally responsible for them." Embodied in this term *koinonea* is the core definition of a gang!

A program in Boston called God's Posse incorporates many of the positive aspects of gang life in its work with youthful offenders. As a result, many youth choose to follow Christian teachings and leave destructive gangs.

Likewise, the aftercare homes of Straight Ahead Ministries are structured around the same concepts. With input from the youth, a Covenant of Commitment has been designed for every-one to sign (see Appendix A). Each person is asked to speak truthfully about his or her life and commits to do the same for others. Not everyone in these homes has been ready for this or has wanted it. But for those who have chosen to sign, the covenant has helped youth develop more character and maturi-ty than almost any other component of the program. Nearly every major issue that has surfaced in the lives of children and has ultimately been resolved has been because of a mutual com-mitment to *koinonea*.

Children of Exile

Children need strong cultural and spiritual foundations to develop personal identity and values. The loss of common cultural identity and spiritual values leaves children adrift in a hedonistic and materialistic society without roots or a compass. This subculture of anomie provides neither the essential foundation for a conscience nor a sense of purpose and hope.

Love Is a Tattoo

Sixteen-year-old Laura had already lived for 3 years on the streets, with no positive adults involved in her life. When we first met her in jail, she had L-O-V-E tattooed on her knuckles. She bragged that she had pierced nearly every part of her body.

She had tried to survive by panhandling. She protected herself with an aura of toughness, making it clear that she hated all men. Though she had had many sexual encounters, she stated that in her entire life she had made love only once. When asked if she trusted anyone, she thought for awhile and then said solemnly, "Yes, I had a cat once that I could tell anything to."

She was proud of the fact that she was in jail for brutally attacking a street man who was rumored to have abused his girlfriend. Laura despised her own absent father and had little contact with her mother. This homeless girl, a thousand miles from her mother, had nobody to take the time to nurture her or heal her wounds. When people saw her physical demeanor, they quickly looked away and crossed to the other side of the street, just as the priest had in the parable of the good Samaritan.

She was very guarded toward us until we asked if there was anything she needed. Shyly, she admitted that she had been locked up for four months but still did not have any socks. We assured her we would have some sent to her. After the visit, Laura seemed more like a little girl, ending the visit by asking, "Will you come to see me again?" Still she was ambivalent in spiritual discussions. Hating her earthly father, how could she trust a heavenly one?

CHAPTER 5

Pathways to Trouble
the making of a delinquent

*The greatest difficulty of human science is the education
of children. It is no hard matter to get children, but after
they are born, then begins the trouble.*
   —Michel de Montaigne, French educator (1533–1592)

TROUBLED BEHAVIOR usually results from a combination of
environmental factors, personal weakness, and harmful
decision making. It also follows different pathways. Some problems are temporary and self-limiting; other troubled behavior is
chronic and persists for years.

Temporary, Situational Problems

Temporary problems can occur at any stage of growth and
usually are self-limiting. It should be stressed that most youths,
particularly boys, engage in some isolated delinquent acts without becoming career delinquents. A University of Michigan
study showed that 90% of college males had committed some
illegal act which, had they been apprehended, would have
labeled them as a delinquent.[1]

A common delinquency of many otherwise normal girls is
isolated shoplifting, which is usually a passing phase corrected
by guilt, even if a child is not caught. For example, a child steals

candy, but her fear of being caught or displeasing her parents causes her to stop such behavior.

With boys, delinquent activity spikes at adolescence when the sudden surge of hormones causes many to act in boisterous and foolhardy ways. This is not surprising because the testosterone level in a 14-year-old boy shoots up to a level 800% greater than when he was younger. A boy's brain is not yet well equipped to manage this chemical that fuels both sex and aggression. As Australian youth researcher Steve Biddulph puts it, "testosterone has the capacity to make a boy a complete man or a complete idiot!"[2]

Meanwhile, in young girls, rising estrogen levels make them increasingly aware of their sexuality. But estrogen actually helps the brains of girls become better connected than those of maturing boys. As a result, girls are better able to monitor and inhibit their emotions during adolescence.

Beginning in middle school, most children challenge limits and act in ways contrary to the teachings of their parents. This is caused by the growing need for autonomy from parents and strong attachments to peers. Most of these youthful indiscretions are only temporary and will not persist. Surprisingly, even in the case of teens arrested for violent acts, nearly all will not repeat such behavior.

Youth are immensely malleable, and we should not fall into the "assume the worst" thinking error, stigmatizing them forever. *Still, all acts of irresponsible behavior should be taken seriously.* To explain such acts away is to signal acceptance of antisocial behavior. Such incidents offer crucial opportunities to help youth learn from their mistakes and mature in character development.

Chronic, Escalating Problems

Chronic misbehavior that starts in early childhood and escalates over the years is a common element in the backgrounds of criminals. Problems can even begin in early childhood with small children who are constantly allowed to have their own way.

Undisciplined or "spoiled" children learn that they will get what they want if they cry or throw a tantrum. Infants have no other option to meet their needs, whether they need to be fed, changed into a clean diaper, held, or burped. But if the pattern continues beyond the toddler stage, a child will not learn to delay his or her desire for gratification or respect the needs of others. Sigmund Freud described this problem with the catchy term, "His Majesty, The Baby." Such a child grows up thinking the world exists only for his or her sake.

For example, Billy does not like to hear "No" for an answer. So he screams at the top of his lungs. Not wanting to hear Billy's screams or to be embarrassed by a scene, his parents give in to his demands. Billy learns how to use negative means to get what he wants. Often he is not even angry while he is yelling, screaming, and pounding the floor. He has simply learned how to *use* anger to get what he wants.

Some children do not grow out of problems. Instead, they develop entrenched coping strategies of self-defeating behavior. They move beyond childish crying or tantrums to using deceit, rebellion, coercion, thrill-seeking, vengeance, or retreat. We highlight these six common pathways to serious trouble and the progression of each below.

1. Deceit

Some children learn to get what they want through covert behavior. For example, they may find that lying, cheating, and stealing without consequences are more effective ways of meeting their needs than honesty. At certain ages, all children experiment with lying, but they soon learn that this behavior erodes the trust of loved ones.

When lying persists, however, a child's negative behavior quickly escalates. The inverted triangle below shows that large numbers of children engage in minor covert behavior like lying and shoplifting around age 8 when they figure out that adults cannot run their lives. Most children shortly discard this behavior. Otherwise, they may escalate to property damage in the middle school years. Again, most desist but a very few advance to serious property offenses in adolescence.

THE PATHWAY OF DECEIT

Early Childhood: Hiding things they have broken, taking food or money from home

Middle Childhood: Shoplifting, chronic lying

Pre-adolescence: Vandalism, fire setting, theft

Adolescence: Burglary, auto theft

In a world of adult lies, it is not surprising that children may develop the pattern of lying without apparent guilt. Even when irrefutable evidence is laid out before them, many refuse to back down. They stick to their lies as if they actually believed them.

Distrustful and suspicious parents seem to fuel distrustful and deceitful behavior in their children. Regardless of how deceit begins, when parents and children cannot trust one another, family cohesiveness is destroyed. Research confirms that distrust between youth and parents is 19 times more predictive of family disunity than divorce.[3] Truly, trust is the glue that holds together all successful relationships.

A caring adult needs to develop a significant relationship with a deceitful child if the child is to learn the basics of successful relationships. The adult must communicate a central message: "I will try to always be straight with you, and I want to be able to trust you as well." While trust is incremental and must be earned, we must demonstrate a willingness to trust youth, even if only in small ways, if they are willing to unlearn the pattern of deceit.

2. Rebellion

THE PATHWAY OF REBELLION

Early Childhood: Temper tantrums, resisting correction

Middle Childhood: Naughtiness, disobedience

Pre-adolescence: Persistent challenges
to authority

Adolescence: Truancy,
school suspension

Most parents do not want blindly obedient children who cannot think for themselves or stand up to negative peers. But there is scarcely a more difficult path than that of parenting a strongly rebellious child. While it sometimes seems easier to just ignore a rebellious youth, this only signals to the young person that we have given up on him or her. It tells the child we do not care enough to keep confronting his or her actions. The difficulty comes in knowing which areas to confront and which ones to let slide.

To many, the terms youth and rebellion seem almost interchangeable. While nearly every young person exhibits some form of rebellion, children rebel for different reasons. Thus, it is very important to understand why a young person might be rebelling, for that will affect the type of response we should make. We will consider three types of rebels: antagonistic to authority, strong-willed temperament, and circumstantial rebellion.

Antagonistic to Authority

For some youth, any authority figure brings out the worst in them. This hatred for authority is usually prevalent in young people when the first authority figure, a father or mother, is either absent, rejecting, or abusive. Consequently, when a teacher says, "Sit down," they stand up. They hate the principal, the coach, and the police. They come to hate their boss at work, their probation officer, or anyone who becomes an authority figure in their life.

Scott Larson relates his experience with such youth:

> When we began taking boys into our home who were coming out of prison, I remember being confused and wondering, "Why did they like me when I visited them in jail, but suddenly began to dislike me once we took them into our home?" I would sometimes ask if anything was wrong, if I had offended them in some way.
>
> They would say, "No," for even they did not understand why their feelings toward me had changed. In time I began to realize that it is normal for a young person to subconsciously transfer the hatred held toward the role of a "father" onto anyone who begins to fill that role.

Simply applying more structure, authority, and controls to this type of child only makes the problem worse. Instead, a new and deeper relationship with a parent, or parental figure, must be developed. Only as this relationship improves will the child be able to begin respecting other forms of authority. These young people are living proof of the equation: "Rules minus Relationship equals Rebellion." If they are not bonded to adults, these youngsters can easily progress to serious antisocial behavior.

Strong-Willed Temperament

While nearly every child exhibits some form of rebellion, there are some who seem to be more difficult and less cooperative, almost from birth. Perhaps it is due to a constitutional difference in temperament or a greater need for autonomy. Psychologist James Dobson calls them "strong-willed children." It is a good description, for it suggests that rebellion redirected can be a strength rather than a flaw. And often, we find that our brightest children refuse to be controlled by anybody.

When we go nose-to-nose with a strong-willed child, nobody wins these power struggles. While we do not want to crush the child's spirit, neither can the adult abdicate authority.

The maturity of the child will influence the adult's response, but capitulating to tantrums is counterproductive at every age. When possible, seek to redirect the energies of strong-willed youngsters by cultivating their positive leadership abilities.

We often tell strong-willed youth that we need them to help us to get through to their friends or maintain control in a group, saying, "They'll listen to you more than to me." This empowers them to do good. Almost every time we have asked, "Can you help me by getting the group to be quiet and attentive during our meetings?" they respond, "Sure, no problem. I'll take care of them."

Sometimes it is helpful to give responsibilities to youth who are troublemakers, for they often rise to our level of expectations. In peer-helping programs, we view them as "young staff," tapping into their power, rather than trying to fight it. Volunteer activities can be very helpful in this regard. At the Black Hills Seminars training sessions for professional youth workers, groups of delinquent youth are invited to share their experiences in treatment. Their powerful stories evoke respect from adults, and the youth learn to respond in kind.

Circumstantial Rebellion

Circumstantial rebellion is not as much rooted in the personality of the young person as in the struggles going on around him or her at a particular time. As irrational as this young person may appear, there is usually a specific situation causing the behavior. Try to understand the pressures the youth may be experiencing from his or her perspective. Anxieties, guilt, depression, fear of failure, insecurity, traumas, or strained friendships can all contribute to a youth's state of rebellion.

When it appears that outside influences are negatively influencing a young person, it is important to work primarily on the relationship, keeping comments and advice brief. Often, children cannot even verbalize what is stressing them, but if they sense that you are on their side and not against them, then you can begin working on the situation together.

In some cases, however, particularly where destructive behavior is involved, it is important to voice your concerns. Say something like, "I'm concerned about you, but I'm not sure what role I should play in this. I really care about you and want to help. What do you think would be most useful for me to do or not to do?" This also keeps our relationship from becoming the focus of strain and conflict.

3. Coercion

THE PATHWAY OF COERCION

Early Childhood: Hitting playmates, fighting with siblings

Middle Childhood: Minor aggression, bullying, annoying others

Pre-adolescence: Frequent fighting, combativeness, gang fights

Adolescence: Violence, rape, assault, strong-arm robbery

Some children learn early in life that they can get their way by coercion. A child who continues in this pattern of intimidating others soon becomes a bully. Early intervention with bullies is crucial. Bullying prevention expert John Hoover has noted that those who are "identified as bullies by age 8 are six times more likely to be convicted of a crime by age 24."[4]

One of the obvious differences between incarcerated youth today and those of decades past is their size. Years ago, they tended to be large-framed and physically strong. That is no longer the case. With today's easy access to guns, bullies no longer need to depend on their size.

Thirteen-year-old Tyrone's feet could barely touch the floor as he sat on his chair. He was telling, with great animation, how he had a child pinned to the ground and shaking. "I held a gun to his head and told him, 'I got the power to take your life, or to give it back to you. . . . I'm gonna let you live.'"

John Hoover found that sexist intimidation is a common problem in Midwestern schools. Bullies often lead groups of boys to harass girls, typically picking on those who are either unattractive or more sexually mature. They also launch cruel attacks on other boys who are physically smaller, or who prefer art or music to sports. In general, any youth who appears unlikely to fight back becomes a likely target. They push weaker children around, calling them demeaning names like "sissy" or "faggot."[5]

Girls also bully, but their approach is usually more psychological, such as organizing peers to ostracize one individual. We are encountering more and more girls who physically bully, but they are usually reacting to physical or sexual abuse in their own lives.

Boys who are bullies desperately need caring male models who can be assertive without being aggressive, because bullies often try to prove their masculinity by dominating others. Girls also need this type of role model in men and women. Success in stopping bullying is a three-front engagement targeting the silent majority who look on, the bully, and the victim, as we will discuss in more depth in Chapter 8.

4. Thrill-Seeking

THE PATHWAY OF THRILL-SEEKING

Early Childhood: Is restless, hyperactive

Middle Childhood: Is impulsive, a dare-devil; takes chances

Pre-adolescence: Steals for the thrill; tries drugs, early sexuality

Adolescence: Addictions, promiscuity, daring crimes

A hundred years ago, social worker Jane Addams wrote that the biggest difference between delinquents and other youth was that delinquents had a greater need for adventure. Psychologists since then have found that many troubled youth seem unable to settle into tranquil lifestyles. They find it boring to stay home, to talk with adults, to have a hobby. Boys in particular often display reckless bravado and pursue excitement and stimulation, which often leads to delinquency.

There is evidence that some youth are less fearful of pain or have brains that crave high levels of stimulation. Some of this is developmental, for not many adults love high-decibel music, flying through space on skateboards, and bungee jumping. But often excitement is really a diversion from the pain of intolerable thoughts and inner conflicts.

Youth cannot "thrill away" their problems, and ultimately the pursuit of wild pleasure leads to a sense of great emptiness. The goal in reaching these youths is to find alternative, socially acceptable avenues to excitement. Sports, high-adventure activities, and musical groups can all captivate high-spirited youth. Jane Addams was one of the founders of the American Playground Association, an effort to bring healthy recreation to urban youths.

Effective mentors with at-risk youth do not usually draw them in with merely the offer of a relationship. Initially, youth become interested by the chance to participate in some high-interest activity. But adults in this fast-paced culture also need to show youth how to slow down to help them learn to live with their inner selves.

One teacher in an alternative school classroom ends each week with students gathering together, listening to soft music, and thanking those who have helped them during the week. We all need quiet times to refocus. For persons of faith, reflective prayer and meditation have always been powerful antidotes to the empty cacophony of the pleasure-pursuing world.

5. Vengeance

THE PATHWAY OF VENGEANCE

Early Childhood: Destructive to toys and pets

Middle Childhood: Victim of scapegoating and bullying; feels unfairly treated or disrespected

Pre-adolescence: Fantasizes about getting justice; cruelty to animals, may become a bully

Adolescence: Plans or plots to get back at people; may direct anger at others, harbor deep hatred, or be suicidal (thoughts, threats, or attempts)

Typical of youth in this fifth category of delinquency are those who were responsible for most of the school killings in America in the 1990s. The perpetrators were generally not the typical delinquent—youth from broken homes and high-crime neighborhoods. Instead, they were more typically mainstream youth, often from two-parent families.

What provokes such aggression and violence from these youth? For some, it begins with abuse or rejection by parents or other significant adults. It may also be related to constant ridicule and rejection by peers. When a person no longer feels capable of tolerating humiliation and disrespect, he or she is capable of great violence.

Children who feel secure and loved are better able to tolerate teasing and ridicule. Those who feel worthless and rejected will tend to react to the slightest affront with vengeance and rage. This is why many troubled youth come to believe that protecting their sense of self-respect may be more important than preserving their own lives. There's a fine line between violence against others and self-destruction in these youth. One youth who was locked up for plotting a massacre of his tormentors in school told us, "If I could have killed a dozen of them, it would have been worth giving up my own life."

Some of the cruelest and most frightening acts of violence are the result of deep hatred and bitterness. James Gilligan of the Center for the Study of Violence at Harvard University found vengeance to be a common theme in the violent acts of many offenders.[6] To the person who feels humiliated, rejected, or ridiculed, violence is an attempt to fight back and even the score. In the private logic of a person who feels violated, getting revenge is justice. One of the youths who killed a number of his fellow students justified his actions this way: "I killed because people like me are mistreated everyday. My whole life I felt outcasted and alone. I finally had to do something about it."[7]

6. Retreat

Children who are troubled respond in one of two ways. Some externalize their pain, while others internalize it. The first five pathways describe patterns of acting out. In contrast, children who retreat internalize their conflicts and pain. Their journey down the pathway of retreat is revealed in different ways at different ages:

THE PATHWAY OF RETREAT

Early Childhood: Excessive fearfulness or shyness

Middle Childhood: Worries; cries easily; physical symptoms such as headaches, stomachaches, or fatigue

Pre-adolescence: Dramatic changes in weight or sleep patterns; speaking in affectless monotone; irritability and unhappiness

Adolescence: Eating disorders, dramatic weight gain or loss; drug or alcohol abuse; depression and hopelessness; suicide attempts[8]

Albert E. Trieschman (1931–1984) was one of the first to recognize that the core problem of many troubled children is profound sadness.[9] Some children have suffered so many losses that they are "cried out"—unwilling or unable to handle any more sadness. Some losses may be obvious, such as the death of a friend or family member. Many are small losses that accumulate and overwhelm a child. These children desperately need adults who can help them develop the courage to master loss and sadness in the circumstances of their daily lives.

Experts estimate that as many as 1 in 20 American preteens and adolescents suffer from clinical depression.[10] Juvenile detention centers are filled with children who otherwise would have been placed in mental health facilities before cutbacks eliminated so many of those options. Currently, 1 in 4 teens in the custody of many juvenile institutions are on psychiatric medication.[11]

If one examines the perpetrators of recent school violence for patterns, two common denominators quickly emerge: they were victims of bullying, and they suffered from depression.[12] Internalized pain stays hidden for only so long. Without effective intervention, the effect is cumulative and eventually erupts. And when it does, the results can be more devastating than the behavior in any of the other five pathways to trouble.

Altering the Trajectories to Trouble

While research documents these six pathways toward trouble, the inverted triangles illustrate the fact that only a small number of youth continue lifestyles of deceit, rebellion, coercion, thrill-seeking, vengeance, and retreat. Most are like the prodigal son who "came to himself" and turned away from the wide road to destruction. What can concerned adults do to ensure that fewer youth progress to the more devastating stages of these pathways to trouble? The second part of this book focuses on how we can help troubled youth change the pathways of their lives.

Part Two

The
Road
Home

CHAPTER 6

Courage for the Discouraged
a fresh model for reclaiming

We can either smother the divine fire of youth, or we may feed it. We may either stand stupidly staring as it sinks into a murky fire of crime and flares into the intermittent blaze of folly, or we may tend it into a lambent flame with power to make clean and bright our dingy city streets.

—Jane Addams, American social worker (1860–1935)

THE MODERN JUVENILE COURT was born in 1899 in a building across the street from the Hull House in Chicago where Jane Addams worked with immigrant families and their often wayward youths. She believed that the answer to most delinquency problems could be found in cultivating the spirit of youth rather than treating them as unredeemable criminals. In that era, troubled youth were often described as "discouraged," and the solution was seen as rekindling their courage.

For thousands of years, philosophers like Plato, Thomas Aquinas, and Paul Tillich have all tried to define courage. The dictionary defines courage as "the state or quality of mind or spirit that enables one to face danger, fear, or vicissitudes with self-possession, confidence, and resolution."[1] But even gang members and bullies may display this type of courage.

We use the word *courage* in a much deeper way than a surface dictionary definition, defining it as "acting with strength and integrity even in the face of life's most difficult challenges." It is interesting that the word *encourage* means *to inspire courage.* Saint Paul actually used this concept as a paradigm for nurturing authentic faith when he wrote, "We dealt with each of you as a father deals with his own children, *encouraging*, comforting and urging you to live lives worthy of God" [emphasis added].[2]

By the mid-twentieth century, however, the term *courage* had been replaced by the more psychological concept of *self-esteem.* Although self-esteem is a useful idea in behavioral research, it has been watered down in popular usage to mean almost anything that produces a "feel good" response.

We recall attending a conference where people were asked to stand on chairs and chant vapid mantras like "I love me! I am wonderful!" What a grossly distorted sense of self-esteem. Inflated self-esteem that does not reflect a positive and productive lifestyle is of little value. For example, studies show that American students have higher academic self-esteem but have lower achievement than Japanese students. Likewise, bullies tend to possess better self-esteem than their victims. Feeling puffed up about performing poorly is maladjustment, not mental health.

In contrast to these superficial views, a large body of solid research indicates how children actually develop positive self-esteem and self-worth. Paul Tillich in his classic book, *The Courage to Be*, explains how hardship and courage are often directly related. He points out that without courage no young person can overcome obstacles. On the other hand, young people are unlikely to acquire real courage apart from experiencing hardship. Thus, disadvantaged youths may actually have an advantage when it comes to developing the attribute of courage—as long as they have access to someone who can instill in them some of the essential building blocks for healthy development.

The Circle of Courage

Four qualities are essential for the development of courage. Youngsters who lack courage are at risk of failing in school and life. But youth who possess them are far better equipped to meet life's challenges.

1. **Belonging:** The universal human longing for love is nurtured by relationships of trust with significant persons in our life. ("I am loved.")

2. **Mastery:** Our inborn thirst for learning is nurtured as we gain understanding and competence in coping with the world. ("I am good at something.")

3. **Independence:** Our desire to exercise free will is nurtured by increased responsibility. ("I have power to make decisions.")

4. **Generosity:** Our passion for life is nurtured by concern for others and commitment beyond one's self. ("I have a purpose for my life.")

Beyond basic safety and survival, we believe these four needs are absolutely essential to healthy youth development. They are shown in the following drawing, entitled *The Circle of Courage.*[3]

GENEROSITY

INDEPENDENCE   **BELONGING**

MASTERY

Youth who are deprived of opportunities for belonging, mastery, independence, and generosity are children of discouragement. They have broken circles. Their problems reflect their discouragement.

The philosopher Mortimer Adler contends that one of the common errors in modern thought is the belief that there are no absolute values or truths. Certainly many values do reflect our cultural differences or personal preference. But Adler argues that there are absolute values, which are true in any place or culture or time. What makes these values universal is the fact that humans have all been created with the same basic needs.

Belonging, mastery, independence, and *generosity* are universal values, rooted in universal human needs. Yet millions of children are dependent on adults who deprive them of opportunities to experience love, to learn, to become responsible, or to find a purpose for living. Adults who are indifferent to these needs are violating children just as surely as those who actively abuse them.

FOUNDATIONS OF COURAGE	PROBLEMS OF DISCOURAGEMENT
Belonging	Alienation and rejection
Mastery	Failure and frustration
Independence	Helplessness and defiance
Generosity	Selfishness and indifference

Behavioral scientists use the more technical terms of *attachment, achievement, autonomy,* and *altruism* to describe the four universal needs underlying *belonging, mastery, independence,* and *generosity*. Research suggests these needs are so essential to human well-being that they are fundamental building blocks in our genetic makeup. We sometimes refer to these God-given qualities as the human resilience code. But although these virtues are created in our *nature*, they cannot flower without *nurture*. John Seita, himself a former troubled youth, said that the job description for all adults is to be "child gardeners," planting and cultivating young lives. We turn now to that task.

Nurturing Belonging

In his book, *The Return of the Prodigal Son*, Henri Nouwen writes, "Trust is that deep inner conviction that the Father wants me home."[4] Attachments develop in a child's earliest bonds with caregivers. When attachments are secure, children develop a healthy sense of belonging. Children who do not feel wanted usually have difficulty trusting others. As a result, they easily become disheartened, discouraged, and dejected—not just about a few specific things, but about life in general. Longing for love, they are at the same time deathly afraid of it.

Daring to Trust

Victor was well-protected against adults. Every time we started getting *too close* to him, he would reveal his philosophy: "I've been hurt so many times, that I'll hurt you before you have a chance to hurt me." Youth like Victor have a not-so-subtle way of sabotaging every significant relationship they enter. Their fear of being hurt becomes a self-fulfilling prophecy that leads them to conclude, "See, I knew you'd just leave me like all the others."

When we learned more about Victor's family background, we found that he had never known his father. And the first thing he recalls about his mother is her saying, "I wish you had never been born." Knowing his mother, we doubt she would ever remember making such a statement. But Victor does, and it continues to haunt him even as a young adult. He needs one person who will stay with him long enough to redefine his image of a parental figure.

Not only do young people need significant adult role models, they need positive peer relationships as well. But sometimes peers bring out the worst in one another. Parents often complain about "those kids" their son or daughter hangs out with who are a bad influence. Such friendships are frequently not the result of a child succumbing to peer pressure. Young people who do not trust adults gravitate to friends with whom they feel comfortable and accepted.

Daring to Choose Positive Peers

Youth with a broken sense of belonging will often pursue substitute attachments. They are vulnerable to offers of acceptance from persons who will use or misuse them. They are easily misled and tend to fall into destructive friendships which only fuel further distrust.

Melanie lived in a trailer park and saw herself as a downscale kid in a generally upscale school. She was so shunned or ignored by most of her peers that she became euphoric when Karen, whom she saw as a "popular" girl, reached out to her as a friend. Karen's father owned a national chain of fashionable clothing stores and lived in the finest part of the city. But Melanie soon discovered that Karen's idea of friendship was merely for a "huffing" companion, someone she could get high with on any kind of aerosol spray she could find in her collection of beauty products.

Melanie shares her experience in her own words:

> I met Karen's parents and they were wonderful. She had everything I didn't and I could never figure out why she wanted to hang with me or do drugs. I didn't really want to huff, but she was my only friend. Eventually Karen's parents admitted her into a drug treatment program.
>
> I realized then that Karen was a false friend. Now I know that just because someone has money or popularity doesn't mean I should sell myself out for them. That's helped me to be a lot more selective in who I hang around with. Now I don't care so much about being the most popular kid in school. I've found a friend who is more like a sister to me—and we would never do anything to hurt each other.

Nurturing Mastery

"Train up a child in the way he should go, and when he is old he will not depart from it," says the writer of Proverbs.[5] Children need knowledge, skills, and values to confront the challenges of living and to creatively solve problems. Those without competence become locked into patterns of self-defeating behavior and develop a failure identity.

Competence is essential for developing a sense of mastery. A person without competence lacks the skills for success in school and life. With a deep sense of mastery, one feels that "Whatever problem the world brings, I can overcome it. Whatever problem I face, I can solve it." Mastery, properly understood, displays a sense of confidence and humility, not arrogance and pride.

Unrealized, a person feels incompetent, inferior, or just plain ineffective. Rather than having a sense of sway over his or her environment, this person feels mastered and manipulated by it. All efforts can seem futile. This young person can begin to develop a *failure complex*.

Most at-risk youth have experienced so much failure in their young lives that they no longer believe they can succeed at anything. In fact, many of them begin to subtly feel more comfortable failing than they do succeeding. Success is scary. Failure is at least familiar.

Repeatedly, we have seen kids purposely fail or be kicked out of programs just days before graduation. For many of them, successfully completing something places even greater pressure on them. If people suddenly start believing in them, they will be expected to continue succeeding. This is a paralyzing thought for a child who feels incapable or unworthy of success. In the eyes of many youth, this newly found success could only be short-lived. They see it as a setup for an even greater fall in the future.

The Courage to Succeed

Not long ago, we saw Billy back in the detention center where we had seen him many times over the past 3 years. "What happened this time, Billy?"

"I don't know. I guess I was just doing *too* good," he responded.

"Too good? That's a new one. People don't usually end up back in here for doing too good," we countered.

"Well, I was back in school, I had a job, and things were really coming together. My family was proud of me . . . for the first time I can remember. Then I just started getting scared. I knew I wouldn't be able to keep it up, and eventually I was going to crash and disappoint everybody. So I figured I might as well just do it now, before I had too much to lose."

Failure complexes can run so deep. It is not surprising that one of the most common tattoos worn in adult prisons is simply, *Born to Lose.*

The quest to be competent, to do things well, is part of our human nature. But the desire to prove ourselves superior to others is more a byproduct of a dominator-driven culture. Children who buy into the mentality of "I win—you lose" will never be truly confident in the sense of their own worth and competence.

While many youths take pride in sloppiness, others, particularly girls, almost kill themselves trying to be perfect and popular. Driven by irrational ideas of "I'm not as good as others" or "I must be the best," even bright girls can develop incredibly destructive behavior. A middle school boy's flippant comment, "Hey Fatso," can set a young girl on the ruinous track of anorexia.

Research shows that many youths feel stupid, do not like the way they look, and feel socially and intellectually incompetent even in the face of evidence to the contrary. The Austrian psychiatrist Alfred Adler popularized the term *inferiority complex* to describe persons who constantly compare themselves to others and feel they do not measure up. Comparing ourselves to others always leaves us coming up on the short end.

Of course, the media play an enormous role in perpetuating this sense of insecurity. In 1995, 3% of the girls on the island of Fiji suffered from bulimia. That was the year television arrived. Just 3 short years later, the rate of bulimia among teenage girls had jumped to 17%.[6] More than ever before, adults are faced with the tremendous responsibility of helping young people gain a deeper appreciation for the unique persons they were created to be.

Reclaiming Cultural Roots

Kaila was a Native American girl whose parents had died in an alcohol-related accident. She was adopted at age 5 by a white family. She got along well at home but from the time she entered school in a white suburban neighborhood, Kaila struggled to feel she measured up to other kids. "I used to be smart," she says, fondly remembering some of her teachers. "But then I quit being smart and I hated school." After third grade, she would never speak in class for fear she might sound dumb.

Though strikingly attractive, Kaila came to believe she was ugly. Hunting for the tiniest pimple, she would try to excise it with a pair of tweezers. She hid from the sun for fear that her skin would become even darker. She curled her hair like the white girls and tried to imitate their version of "Valley Girl" talk. Hearing older boys call her "prairie nigger" (a racist slur used against Plains Indians) would send her into a depression for days.

One day Kaila overheard some boys making fun of a girl who supposedly "had the biggest butt in the class." She measured hers and became obsessed with the idea that she had to lose weight. She would run extra laps in gym and try to consume only soda and cigarettes, all to no avail.

Soon she found a friend with a similar hobby of weight loss. Together they had a contest to see who could lose the most weight. "But we liked food too much and would always relapse," she said. "So we invented a 'puking contest' by pigging out and then seeing who could throw up the most."

When her friend received counseling and quit purging, Kaila was even more depressed. "I guess I should have been glad because it probably saved her life, but all I could think of was that no friend wanted me. I am dumb and unpopular."

Kaila needed to learn that she did not have to be brilliant or perfect to be loved. We explained to her that in her Native culture, children always tried to better their *own* performance rather than try to prove they were better than others. She shared that she had lacked any racial pride because the only members of her race she knew had hurt her.

We paired her with a mentor who was a professor of Native American studies, and she became fascinated with Forrest Carter's book, *The Education of Little Tree,* an account of an orphaned Indian youth raised in traditional ways by his Cherokee grandparents. Through her mentor, Kaila began to reclaim her rich heritage. She is now planning to be a counselor for Native American children: "I want them to discover their roots."

Nurturing Independence

The parable of the prodigal son is a story of a youth who believes he can find freedom without responsibility. The Bible always refers to undisciplined passion as enslavement. As the younger son discovered, escape from his father's influence was not freedom at all. Freedom is the power to do right. And for true freedom to exist, self-discipline and responsibility must be nurtured. As children learn to make good decisions, they are equipped for successful independence. Children who lack responsibility are easily misled, or they may rebel in a false independence.

Personal power, or "empowerment," manifests itself as fruitful self-control and self-regulation. While it is often referred to as independence or autonomy, power is only healthy if developed within the context of deep relational belonging. In fact, power emerges directly out of embracing relationships. Consequently, it may appear as willfulness or stubbornness when a young person attempts to take over the decision-making and authority roles previously held by loved elders.

Responsibility, developed in an individual, however, produces the ability to make prudent decisions even in the face of compelling outside pressures. Undeveloped, a person will feel powerless and will harbor strong suspicions of self-doubt.

Adolescents are in a precarious period of their lives. One moment they appear confident and self-assured, and the next moment they are hopelessly insecure. They are at a stage where they need to make their own decisions, yet at times they must be protected from their own destructive choices. What is commonly known as rebellion most often surfaces during this transition period when they begin to enjoy some of the freedom of responsible adults, yet are still sheltered from some of the risks that come with living independently.

Because of their heightened need for autonomy and individuation, young people tend to define success very differently than the adults who care for them. In the minds of most adults, successful parenting is getting children to *do all the right things* or *not do the wrong things*. Adults will say, "Don't hang around with that crowd." "Say no to drugs and alcohol." "Do your schoolwork." If by some miracle, we can get them to do all the right things . . . *we've succeeded!*

The only problem is that even if young people do what we want—do not go to that party, do their homework, do not date that boy or girl, stay away from the wrong crowd, come home on time, etc.—they feel that they have failed if they did not make these decisions on their own. Youth would rather make the wrong decisions but have them truly be their decision.

"Being my own person"

Jason had been locked up for 4 years and had just moved into the Larsons' home. After a few months, he began to get into some trouble with friends, so his activities were restricted for a time.

For a couple of weeks, he could not go out except for school, work, or with somebody else from the house. During that time, we observed that it was particularly difficult to wake him up in the morning. Jason was always tired, but this did not make any sense to us because he was at home now more than ever.

One day, after Jason's grounding was over, he said, "You probably noticed how tired I was during the past few weeks."

"Yes, we certainly did notice. Why were you so tired?"

"Well, believe it or not, I would get up at one or two o'clock in the morning, when everyone else was sleeping, and walk around outside."

"Oh, great. What were you doing, hooking up with your old friends?" we asked.

"No. Nobody's out on our street at that time of the night."

"Were you drinking by yourself then?"

"No. I wasn't drinking. I wasn't doing anything. . . I was just walking."

We continued probing. "Well, are you still doing it?"

"No. I don't do it anymore."

"When did you stop?"

"When my grounding was over."

"So, why did you do it, Jason?"

"I don't know. I guess . . . just cause you said I couldn't."

Somehow, in Jason's mind he was succeeding. He was being his own person.

While all youth gravitate to their peers as they gain more independence, sometimes these associations cause them to virtually resign from their families. This is particularly true when peers engage in activities strongly disapproved by parents, such as promiscuous sexuality, delinquency, or alcohol and other drug abuse. The tension between the incompatible value systems of family and friends causes most youth to confine their rebellion to the value framework of their parents. But others make a total break and reject the values their parents had so carefully tried to instill in them.

Finding Real Freedom

A loving family had adopted Rich, who had always been very strong-willed and rebellious. He rejected his father's admonishments to do better in school so that he could get into a good college. Because his mother had difficulty setting firm limits, he easily manipulated her by saying, "You're not my real mother."

Soon Rich was staying out late on weekends and refusing to go to church with the family. When they would bring it up, he would declare he was agnostic and that they were violating his rights. He quit both the church youth group and his Explorer Scout Troop. As home relationships became rocky, Rich spent more and more time away, staying overnight with friends several nights a week.

Unable to lay the law down, his parents felt all of their influence over him slipping from their hands. Hoping absence might make the heart grow fonder, they agreed to let him go to Europe on an exchange program during his junior year. When he returned, it was obvious the trip had not produced what they had hoped.

Rich began accusing his parents of sending him away because they did not want him around. They were furious as well, for the idea had been his in the first place. Soon all communication between Rich and his parents had ceased. At one point, his father even called the police after one of Rich's wild parties made its way into their home, where several items were damaged or stolen to buy drugs.

As a result, Rich was mandated to a drug treatment program. He first relapsed quickly, but after a second stint, he began to stabilize. At 18, he has a sober girlfriend, has a part-time job in a computer store, and is living at home, trying to finish high school. "I want to stay sober and go to college," he explains. He has even begun to hug his parents again. "I know I have hurt them a lot, and I almost lost them completely," he says tearfully. "Now I realize how much they really do love me. I guess I just had to find out the hard way."

His parents struggle with their efforts to determine how much structure to require of an 18-year-old, and how much freedom to give. And they still worry about him when his independent streak flares up from time to time. "We have made it clear to Rich that he's free to leave, with our blessing, at any time," they explain. "But if he wants to stay, then he must abide by the guidelines we agree upon." Rich has experienced enough of the dark side of life that he seems content and appreciative to stay, for now anyway. Perhaps it helps that staying is now his choice.

Rich's parents hope they have been through the worst, and he is constantly in their prayers. More recently, he started going to church with them again, too, and the sparkle is starting to come back in his eyes. Says his mother, "I know the saying that 'the family that prays together stays together.' We are also discovering that it helps to laugh together as well."

Nurturing Generosity

We all need to believe there is some purpose for our lives beyond simple animal survival. Psychologist Viktor Frankl (1905–1997) put it this way: "What man actually needs is not a tensionless state, but rather the striving and struggling for some goal worthy of him." Persons who are self-centered lack a purpose for living and show little empathy or conscience; those who are committed to serving God and others exhibit humble generosity and self-sacrifice.

It is hard to imagine how the virtue of generosity could be distorted, but any good thing can be abused. Gangsters are very generous and loyal to their fellow crooks, but they exploit others. Some people let others exploit their generosity and turn them into slaves out of their own deep need for acceptance or friendship. It is possible to give so much to others that we fail to take care of ourselves. The Golden Rule asks that we show the same concern for others as we show ourselves, but this implies that our own needs should be met if we are to be able to meet the needs of others.

Survivor's Pride

Rebecca and her younger sister, Rondi, lived with their mentally ill mother. Though amicable with neighbors, their mother would often fly into fits of rage and throw objects against the walls. One of the earliest incidents of violence happened when Rebecca was in kindergarten. She had just learned in school about dangerous strangers, so the next morning she cried and begged her mother to accompany her to school so a stranger would not kidnap her.

Frustrated by her inability to stop Rebecca's crying, her mother finally dragged the child into the bathroom where she beat and kicked her. Afterward, she felt sorry and warned Rebecca that if she told, both girls would be sent to different foster homes where cruel people would lock them in dark basements and beat them.

After that, the beatings became much more frequent. Rebecca learned that if she took the blame for whatever went wrong, Rondi could be spared. "When my mother got angry, protecting my little sister became my main job," she explained. Because Rebecca always intercepted her mother's wrath, her mother came to despise her all the more, telling her in no uncertain terms that she was the black sheep of the family. Because her mother worked nights and would come home later and later, Rebecca became the functioning parent for her little sister.

For 6 years, Rebecca covered up her mother's problems, trying desperately to manage her moods so all would be safe. She even read pamphlets about child abuse that had been published by a children's shelter in their city.

Finally her mother lost her job, and the family was evicted from their apartment. The girls were staying in their car one cold night, but their mother did not return. After several hours, 11-year-old Rebecca knew she had to tell somebody. She called the shelter's toll-free number. After an investigation, both girls were put in foster care and now have limited contact with their mother. To this day, her mother tries to make Rebecca feel responsible for destroying the family.

Rebecca had to play the role of rescuer in her family, while her own needs were not met. She is a very generous person almost to the point of a fault. Not surprisingly, she soon gravitated to a troubled boyfriend and tried to rescue him like she had rescued her little sister. Now she is learning to understand the difference between genuine generosity and the distorted generosity of codependency, and she is trying to connect with more stable friends.

Like most survivors, Rebecca still carries some scars and sometimes slips back into wondering why her mother abandoned her. She needs assurance to realize that she is not to blame. We have tried to give her a sense of "survivor's pride," pointing out the remarkable maturity she displayed in the face of very difficult circumstances. Fortunately for Rebecca and Rondi, even if their mother never changes, they have a loving, dedicated foster mother who is a healthy parental role model for them.

While Rebecca is learning not to let people use her, she is still a remarkably generous person. She volunteers at a local homeless shelter, and recently said that she hoped to win the lottery someday so she could buy the local eight-story Holiday Inn and turn it into a homeless shelter: "I would even give good rooms to people who are drunk because it's wrong to just turn them away without any hope."

A Purpose for Living

Survival alone does not give meaning to life. The highest kind of purpose involves self-sacrifice—the giving of oneself to others, the sacrificing of one's own interests for a cause larger than oneself.

But when purposelessness abounds, meaninglessness abounds. This is described by a suicide note found from a New Hampshire teen: "Not having a good enough reason to live is a good enough reason to die."

People who are wrapped up in their own problems need to become less self-centered and contribute to others. Service projects are an important element for youth in their tumultuous adolescent years. In Straight Ahead Ministries' homes for troubled youth, mission trips are one of the most powerful agents for change.

When we asked Michael, who had been with us for nearly a year, which one of the mission trips he might be interested in, none seemed to capture his interest.

"I don't know," he sighed, "I guess I've always kind of wanted to work with disabled people. Is there anything I can do like that?" A friend of ours ran a one-week camp each summer for disabled adults, so we phoned her. She said she needed full-time personal care attendants for each of the attendees, and would be interested in meeting with Michael.

That turned out to be the best week of Michael's life. He called home every day to tell about his adventures with John, a man with autism. When Michael came back home, he said, "You know, this is the first time I've felt like there was a purpose for my life. I think I've finally found what I was made for."

All Kids Are Our Kids

We have often heard teachers and others say, "What can we possibly do? Look at this kid's family!" But simply blaming the family does little good. If the lives of troubled young people are to change, others in the community must become involved and play a role in the lives of individual children.

Nowhere is there more potential for positive influence than in faith-based programs. They are one of the few cross-generational groups that can help rebuild a sense of community. Nearly every other segment of modern society has segregated its young from its older members. Schools, recreational programs, entertainment centers, and even many families keep youth distanced from adults. Traditional faith communities do not. Churches and synagogues are not merely buildings. Ideally, they are communities of committed people who are also potential employers, adult mentors, and positive peer groups—all things that troubled adolescents desperately need.

What are the essential elements provided by adults who live in close proximity with young people? Fortunately, we now have available a solid body of scientific information about what works in the prevention and treatment of delinquency. Children need to be reared in environments that provide opportunities to develop and experience *belonging, mastery, independence,* and *generosity.* This is not just the responsibility of the family. As Peter Benson of the Search Institute in Minneapolis says, "All kids are our kids."

The Search Institute provides communities with a blueprint for creating a positive youth development "infrastructure." An ongoing Search Institute research project involving hundreds of thousands of youth has identified 40 "developmental assets," which are the building blocks of healthy youth development. Half are external assets, such as supportive relationships with parents and teachers and positive expectations for behavior. The other half are internal assets, such as educational competence and positive values. The complete list is included in Appendix B.

When these external supports and inner strengths are present, high-risk behavior is greatly reduced. Youths lacking these assets are at much greater risk for a host of risky behaviors, including substance abuse, sexual activity, school behavior problems, delinquency, eating disorders, and depression or suicide. Surprisingly, in every community studied to date, most youths have less than half of the total developmental assets, and only 1 in 10 met the set of criteria for "optimal healthy development."[7]

Benson concludes that a serious rupture has occurred in our youth development infrastructure. This is not only an inner-city problem but one that affects suburbs and small agricultural communities as well. Every part of the ecology of childhood—home, school, peers, and community—can have a powerful impact on positive youth development. In the terminology of treatment professionals, we need to provide wraparound services tailored to the specific needs of children and families. How can we help our displaced youth find their way home? The rest of this book focuses on the roadmap for these relationships. This includes reparenting, redirecting, reconciling, and redeeming, as shown in the chart below.

FOUNDATIONS OF COURAGE	PROBLEMS OF DISCOURAGEMENT	RECLAIMING SOLUTIONS
Belonging	Alienation and rejection	Reparenting
Mastery	Failure and frustration	Redirecting
Independence	Helplessness and defiance	Reconciling
Generosity	Selfishness and indifference	Redeeming

CHAPTER 7

Reparenting

cultivating trust

Your authority with children is directly proportional to your value as an esteemed adult.
　　—Janusz Korczak, Polish youth advocate (1878–1942)

DEVELOPMENTAL PSYCHOLOGIST ERIK ERIKSON identified the first stage of healthy development as the formation of trusting relationships with primary caregivers. If a child does not develop secure trust at home, the result usually carries over into later relationships. What is needed, then, is a strategy for developing bonds between the youth and significant adults.

Most children who have minor scrapes with authorities in school or in the community eventually mature and go on to positive adult adjustment. But some youth's troubles seem to persist and escalate over the years. In our experience, the majority of youth who get into chronic trouble and delinquency share one or more of these common attributes early in their lives:

- Lack of appropriate structure

- Abuse or neglect

- A sense of loss or abandonment

In this chapter, we look at common problems with the parenting connection and suggest ways of building corrective relationships, either with the child's parents or with other caring adults.

Lack of Appropriate Structure

Webster's dictionary defines rebellion as "the act of resisting or opposing the controls." Just as children have a built-in need to rebel, they also have a built-in need for controls, or boundaries. Obviously, as they grow older, the boundaries need to widen, but no matter where the boundaries are, youth will bounce off them. And once the boundaries are removed, they may "go crazy" for a while. However, they usually move back to where the boundaries were previously placed, as the following illustration shows:

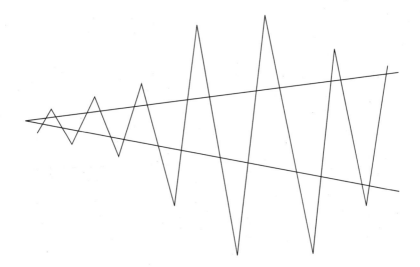

This process of testing and bouncing off stable boundaries is essential for the healthy development of children. In fact, the Search Institute identifies boundaries and expectations as being among the most critical of all adolescent needs. Different supports in the lives of young people can provide healthy boundaries:

- *Families* with clear rules and expectations model positive behavior and monitor the young person's whereabouts.

- *Schools* offer positive expectations when they have clear rules and consequences.

- *Peers* can provide a positive influence and model responsible behavior.

- *Communities* can set expectations with positive adult models and neighbors who take responsibility for monitoring a young person's behavior.

Properly functioning, each level of influence in a young person's life can contribute to a sense of boundaries. But when the boundaries are not clearly set in the home, the next boundaries are usually at school, and children will bounce off these. When limits are not enforced at school, the next boundary is often the law, and children bounce off it. While all children challenge limits, there is nobody more miserable than the child who has no clear sense of boundaries.

Finding Security in Boundaries

Marcus was in a detention center where we were talking about rules. He commented, "I could do anything I wanted growing up. No one ever told me I had to go to school, when I had to be home at night, or anything. No one ever put any rules on me."

"Oh, here we go," we thought, "He's bragging about not having any rules. If only he understood. . . ."

Then Marcus looked down as he continued, "I guess there just wasn't much love in my home."

The opposite of love is not hate; it is indifference. Even angry exchanges communicate on some level that at least a child is noticed, that he or she is in some social bond, however hostile. Careless parenting rooted in indifference is perhaps the most destructive child-rearing process—one that might be more accurately spelled *CARE-LESS*.

Boundaries are not only restrictive; they also provide a sense of security for children. Young people thrive in an atmosphere where the values and expectations are consistent, fair, and predictable. In juvenile penal institutions, it is not uncommon to have a youngster act out or even attempt to escape only days before a scheduled release date. Is it that they wanted to get out so much? No, usually it is the opposite. They fear leaving such a predictable, secure environment, even if it is a lockup setting. This does not mean children are being treated too well in these settings, but rather that they know too well what they need, and they fear adults will not provide this after their release.

One such youth said, "It seems the only time I get any attention is when I get locked up. Then I have people who want to talk to me all day long—counselors, teachers, psychologists, even my parents. Everybody's suddenly very interested in me. And it feels good."

Abuse or Neglect

In a typical year, approximately 3 million cases of suspected child abuse are reported in the United States. Also, each year, approximately 3 million juveniles encounter the police or justice system. Is it coincidental that these numbers are virtually identical? Not likely. According to the Child Welfare League of America, childhood abuse and neglect are the highest indicators of future delinquency.[1]

While child abuse is no excuse for delinquent behavior, we do know that youngsters who are abused often turn the tables and victimize society. Child abuse is the "smoking gun" behind much of youth violence. Studies have shown that abused and neglected youth are 66 times more likely to become early delinquents than other children. For boys alone, a record of abuse increases the likelihood of delinquency by over 100 times. In one study of juvenile murderers on death row, Dorothy Otnow Lewis found that all of her subjects had been abused and, in some cases, tortured by parents and stepparents.[2]

Derrick was a boy in one of Straight Ahead's aftercare homes. He had been abused by his father, and in turn had abused his younger siblings. Wracked with a sense of guilt and shame, Derrick would often say to us, "I'd feel more comfortable if you'd beat me rather than love me." Once he even said, "I want to commit a crime so bad that I will have to go to prison for a long time. Maybe that's how I can pay for all the bad things I've done." Unfortunately, Derrick did just that. Only two weeks after leaving our home, he committed a crime that landed him in an adult prison for 10 years.

Phil Quinn, himself an abused child, has written several books on this topic and is a national advocate for abused youth. He contends that abuse poses a threat to the survival of a child, unlike any experience other than war or torture. Children are thrust prematurely into the adult world of power, violence, and sex where they are forced to find some way to survive. Children are born with a trusting spirit, which he calls "congenital hope," but child abuse makes them feel powerless and vulnerable to death, leading to "congenital despair." They learn to expect the worst from others, but to blame themselves.

The healing process involves building trust with such a child, gradually helping the youngster learn that he or she is a person of great value and is not to blame for what has happened. These children often need counseling to reconcile their anger toward their abuser and even to forgive themselves so that they may feel secure enough to trust others again.

A Sense of Loss or Abandonment

We often ask young people who are in jail, "If you could go back to any point in your life and start over, how far back would you go?" It is amazing how quickly most can pinpoint a specific point in time, a pivotal experience that put their life on a completely different course:

"I would go back to age 12, when my father left home," said one boy.

"I'd go back to when I was 9. That's when my grandmother died, and I quit caring about anything."

"When I was 10. That's when my father went to prison and my mother started doing drugs."

For many troubled girls, that pivotal moment came when their mother's live-in boyfriend began abusing them.

These are all *landmark events* because they change the pathway of a person's life. We gain a better understanding of the trajectory of delinquency by knowing what these landmark events were. But even more important than what happened is how an individual interprets events in his or her private logic. Losing a father to death may make one child more appreciative of the surviving parent, while another may reject all other caregivers lest he lose them as well.

When we consider that one of the most powerful needs of youth is for secure bonds to adults, then the loss of such bonds is potentially the most devastating circumstance a child can encounter. English psychologist Denis Stott studied 102 delinquent boys in thorough interviews over several years. He was surprised to discover that more than half of chronic delinquents had experienced the threat of loss of family. He identified a continuum of behavior problems that are associated with broken attachments.

THE ATTACHMENT CONTINUUM

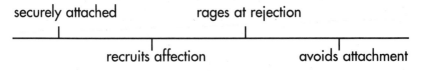

The impact of broken attachments is illustrated in the story of PJ.

PJ Loses His Pop

Harry was a psychologist in an Australian youth correctional facility. When we met at a conference, he asked if we would be willing to meet with him and PJ, a resident in that institution. We readily agreed. PJ had recently been transferred into this high-security youth prison because of his violent behavior in another locked facility.

Unlike most delinquents who are threatened by counselors, PJ seemed hungry for such contact. When we asked about his family, he told us that his mother was only a child herself when he was born, so he had been raised by grandparents. When asked about his natural father, he exclaimed, "Well, I know his name, but I guess he never thought I was worth finding." He blamed himself for both his mother and father's rejection, and rage had set itself deeply into his life. It intensified even more after his grandfather died.

PJ explained that he was an Aboriginal Australian and asked about the tribal people of North America, the Native Americans. We used this interest to explain that in tribal traditions, every boy has several fathers (brothers of a person's father are called father in traditional tribal cultures). PJ seemed intrigued. We suggested that because he had lost both his fathers, maybe he could find another—not by adoption, but by finding someone he could turn to for fatherly advice.

Earlier Harry had indicated that he would be willing to assume such a reparenting role, although his therapy training had taught him to avoid such involvement. We informed PJ that in speaking all over the world, we had never had a psychologist ask us to travel hundreds of kilometers with him to talk with one of his kids as Harry had. "Harry must think you're pretty important," we assured him. PJ began to glow as he listened. "If you're looking for somebody to talk to like a son to a father, you probably don't have to look any farther than Harry."

Upon returning to the United States, we received a letter from Harry reporting that PJ had been coming to his office every day since our meeting. After a few days, he had asked Harry if he could talk with him about his grandfather's (whom he called Pops) death:

> I've never told anybody this before, but right before Pops died, he called out my name two times and hugged me and held me close for a long time. When the hospital discovered our family didn't have enough money for a burial, they put him on a tray in a refrigerator. I was furious because they weren't respecting my Pop!

In the past, people had always punished PJ for his angry behavior, but nobody took the time to find out where it was coming from. Once PJ was able to express his anger source, he began making rapid gains in counseling, enrolled in school, and became very involved in art.

Recently, PJ was transferred to an open residential program, and Harry is working to get him attached to other significant adults. Harry wrote that he was arranging for the chaplain to spend some quality time in PJ's unit "because he needs all the fathers he can get."

The "Reparenting" Concept

When youth are growing up outside the influence of positive adult models, they need *corrective parenting relationships,* which we call *reparenting.* We have used this admittedly strong term to cut to the core of what is needed to reclaim many of our most challenged youth.

For nearly a century, successful workers worldwide have demonstrated that the most effective strategy for connecting with adult-wary youth is through a process of reparenting. Rather than trying to overpower a youth, the adult instead becomes a powerful model. This requires a combination of a *positive relationship* and *authority.* But these twin strategies are alien to most adults because:

1. Many adults try to avoid close attachments, fearing they might foster "dependency." But in their attempt to keep "boundaries" clear, they end up drawing battle lines and building walls.

2. Other adults, particularly counselors, want to avoid exercising any adult authority. As a result, many of these adults are seen as powerless by such youths and become friends without influence.

Modern research shows that both relationships and authority are essential components of successful work with delinquents. Schulman described this a half century earlier in these terms:

The therapist utilizes this originally shallow relationship to establish himself as a trustworthy authority figure who will not exploit the patient. By creating this type of relationship, one is, *in many respects, reconstructing a father-child situation,* the outcome of which is very unlike the delinquent's earlier life experience.[3]

Reparenting involves providing a youth who is not closely attached to adults with bonds to a positive adult. This adult will provide both emotional bonds and positive discipline.

Reparenting can operate in two ways:

1. *Extending the Family.* Supportive adults become significant surrogate parental forces in a youth's life.

2. *Giving Parents a Fresh Start.* Parents are taught skills that enable them to have a more positive influence.

Contemporary society is faced with scores of underparented kids. Most neighbors no longer become involved, contending that these youth are someone else's problem or a job for professionals. Many educators and youth workers try to keep a "professional distance." But an unbonded child will never be reclaimed by an uninvolved adult.

But do children really *want* our help? Will they even listen to us? A major study revealed that while youths go to each other first for advice, they tend not to trust the advice they receive. The youths surveyed said overwhelmingly that they would prefer to go to their parents or other adults first, but they do not believe they have a relationship with them that allows them to talk openly about their problems.[4]

When children become overwhelmed with the problems in their lives, they need others who can help give them perspective—people who can assure them that "this too will pass." In the absence of significant adult relationships, children can only turn to their peers for help with their confusion. But often peers only increase a young person's feelings of distress. Rarely are they able to offer a voice of wisdom and balanced perspective that comes from having *been there*. This is when the listening ear of a caring adult whom the young person trusts is so critically important.

Most teens who give in to irrational or violent behavior say they felt like the world was just caving in on them, like there was no way out. It is at this very point that the majority of youth today feel they have no adult with whom they can talk. Obviously, adult relationships must be forged before this point of crisis for a teen to feel that he or she has an adult ally that can be trusted. And such a relationship requires a significant investment of both time and energy.

Certainly over-involvement with individual children can create problems; thus some organizations rightfully try to prevent "boundary problems" with rules governing relationships beyond the workplace. Employees with integrity honor these limits, but the bureaucratization of the caregiving process has limited the effectiveness of professionals. By assuming that any kind of love is suspect in people-helping professions, we have strayed far from the original ethics of child-care workers.

In 1829, Samuel Hall wrote the following in the first book for training teachers in the United States:

> If you succeed in gaining their love, your influence will be greater in some respects than of parents themselves. It will be in your power to direct them into almost any path you choose . . . to make them kind, benevolent and humane, or, by your neglect they may become the reverse of everything that is lovely, amiable and generous.[5]

By Hall's standard, many of today's professionals have very little influence in the lives of children.

The original word for education is the Latin *educare*, which connotes "caring for, disciplining, and bringing up youth." Under English law, for hundreds of years, teachers have been seen as holding the power of substitute parents under the *in loco parentis* doctrine.

The word for therapy comes from the first therapist, Petroculus, who was a *therapon* to the Greek warrior and leader Achilles. He lived in the same tent with Achilles, listened to his endless complaints, advocated for him against all adversaries, and eventually died in the performance of his duties. How about that for over-involvement?

When did our schools, youth professions, and citizens begin backing away from our responsibility to help parent our children? Who decided that a child is given only one pass at the parent lottery? How could we have missed the realization that children may need other adults in addition to the parents or guardians who participate directly in the parenting process?

Reparenting by Extending the Family

In almost all tribal cultures in the world, the broader community provides strong support to the child's natural parents. From the beginning of time, some mothers have been too immature, too stressed, lacking in parenting skills, or absent through dying young. But always, a safety net of kin would help fill the gap.

In tribal cultures worldwide, aunts and uncles are typically called mother and father, and most gray-haired persons are considered grandparents. Furthermore, parenting extends well into adulthood. Fred Leader Charge, an administrator at Sinte Gleska University on the Rosebud Reservation in South Dakota, describes his own experience: "Both my fathers still call me the Lakota name for boy when they greet me. I have not yet gained the wisdom to be called the Lakota name for man."

Extended families were also common in North America and Europe until just a few generations ago. And while extended families are still common in some ethnic communities, many of the elders are not the stable forces that they once were. In mobile middle-class culture, involved grandparents have become a rarity. More often, grandparents are mere pictures in a photo album.

Without an extended-family support system, it takes valiant superparents to rear responsible children. Theologian Martin Marty points out that throughout history, the tribe was always needed to ensure that the values of a culture were passed on, for the tribe survives even if the parents do not.

Research from the Search Institute indicates that all children should know at least six adults who support their development through connectedness and continuity over a period of years.[6] How can these roles be met? Neighbors, teachers, church members, and other concerned adults can become part of the new tribe, the extended family that reparents our young.

This is even more true today, where less than half of our children are raised with both natural parents. In America's inner cities, it is less than one in five.[7] Yet the roles that both a father and a mother fill are essential for children to develop into healthy adults.

Nobody can replace a missing parent, but it is possible for someone to provide some of the elements of that significant role. The Apostle Paul knew the power of that kind of relationship. In fact, he penned what might well be the most relevant strategy for reaching at-risk youths in his letter to the Corinthians when he told them that although they had 10,000 instructors, they did not have many fathers.[8]

Paul knew that these people did not need just another teacher. Their needs were much deeper. And while Paul could not fulfill this role to great numbers of people, he was willing to be a father to some people in Corinth. How much more is such extended parenting needed today!

Reparenting by Giving Parents a Fresh Start

Reparenting does not happen only when a third party assumes a surrogate parent role; it can also happen when parents change their parenting approach and start over. Effective parenting is a balancing act between the four most common extremes of parenting styles:

1. Emotional distance that weakens parent-child bonds.

2. Emotional smothering that overwhelms and stifles a child.

3. Punitiveness that infuriates or cripples the spirit of a child.

4. Permissiveness that results in an unguided and self-indulgent child.

While most children can compensate for such errors in parenting, sometimes these errors in combination with other stressors can get a child off to a shaky start. We cannot relive the past, but it is never too late for parents who have new skills and maturity to make a new start in reparenting their own children.

Even parents who have played destructive roles in the early life of their child can repair those broken bonds when both parties are receptive. We recently worked with an 18-year-old youth whose father lost custody when the boy was a small child. After a dozen years of rejection by the father and hatred by the son, the two are now reconciled.

Every parent and child has a natural instinctive desire to be reconciled to one another. In the closing passage of the Old Testament prophetic writings, Malachi beautifully reveals the heart of God: "He will turn the hearts of the fathers to their children, and the hearts of the children to their fathers."[9]

WHAT REPARENTING IS *NOT*

1. *Attempting to Replace a Parent.* We will never replace a youth's parents, nor should we attempt to. In fact, it is detrimental to even speak negatively about a kid's parents when they can hear you. They can do it, but you cannot. Nothing will drive a wedge between you and that young person faster.

   Many inadequate parents are doing the best job they know how. Some parents with problem children have done a very good job; they just need *more* support. Rather than tearing down parents, we must build upon the good they have done. Often, it is the community and peers who have influenced the young person negatively, not the parents.

   Gaining credibility with the family is crucial. Without it, parents will often sabotage what you are attempting to do with their child. Sometimes this is out of jealousy; sometimes, because of misunderstanding. Whenever you work with at-risk youths, to be most effective, that work needs ultimately to carry over into their families.

2. *Assuming the Responsibility for a Young Person.* Most at-risk youth have very complicated lives. It is unlikely that you alone will be able to undo all the damage that has been done. As a general rule, you should not get involved in financially subsidizing their needs. You must also realize that you can have reparenting influence without having a young person move into your home. Ideally, there are many people involved in this young person's life—social workers, counselors, family service agencies, or welfare workers, who can also help meet many of their needs.

WHAT REPARENTING *Is*

1. *Offering a Commitment That Goes Beyond Being Just an Authority Figure.* We cannot provide that in a great number of kids' lives, but most at-risk kids desperately need at least one individual (outside of their immediate family) who will fill this role in their lives. It is our job to help find mature adults who feel called and willing to fill this role in the life of one youth. We must be willing to personally play this role in a few kids' lives as well.

2. *Building a Foundation of* Trust *and* Relationship. These are two necessary ingredients if we are to see positive changes take place in the lives of hurting young people. State officials have occasionally questioned whether we have adequate staff supervision in our homes. At times they have encouraged us to move toward a more "structured program" model versus the "family" paradigm we use. But a program, in and of itself, does not make a kid more safe. Trust and relationship are the only things we have to hold kids. Even the most secure prison in the world is not safe without trust and relationships between staff and inmates.

Unless the issue of trust is resolved for youths, they will remain stunted in their emotional and spiritual development. Honesty, consistency, and being a stable presence through both good and bad times are what lay the critical foundation of trust. Our role is not to *fix* kids, but to *be there* for them. And this, over time, will lay a foundation on which others can build relationships of trust as well.

—Scott Larson, *At Risk: Bringing Hope to Hurting Teenagers* (Loveland, CO: Group Publishing, 1999), pages 48–50.

Reparenting With Respectful Discipline

We are reminded that the term *discipline* comes from the core word *disciple*. Discipleship means following and learning from the guidance and example set by an esteemed mentor. Most adults reenact discipline practices learned in their own family and cultural traditions. Autocratic families and cultures reserve respect for persons in power, leading to *authoritarian* discipline. Egalitarian families and cultures strive for mutual respect and produce *democratic* or *authoritative* discipline.

A century of child development research suggests that there have been three discipline methods in the history of parenting:

1. **Power Assertion.** While *authoritative* adults provide guidance to youth, *authoritarian* adults coerce obedience. This "might makes right" approach keeps children stuck on the bottom rung of the moral development ladder.

2. **Love Deprivation.** Because the most powerful need of children is for love, adults can be tempted to withhold love to control behavior. But emotionally blackmailing kids by threatening to withhold love does great damage to the trust essential for positive relationships.

3. **Respectful Reasoning.** Using this method, adults help youth reflect on how their behavior affects themselves and others. By teaching respect and positive values, we enable children to move up the character development ladder to develop self-discipline.

The United States is in a gradual transition from a power-oriented discipline to approaches shaped by democratic principles. A 1924 study of American parents found that *obedience* was the main goal in child-rearing. By 1988, *independence* had moved to first place. But the United States still has a strong ethos of respect for authoritarianism. Because of these values, corporal punishment of school children and boot camps for delinquents are still remnants of centuries of dominator cultures.

Unfortunately, the terms *discipline* and *punishment* are often confused in contemporary society. Physical punishment is defended by some on the basis of Bible verses like Proverbs 13:24: "Those who spare the rod hate their children" (NRSV). However, it is important to consider how the *rod* was viewed in the Hebrew culture of that day. It was an instrument used to guide ignorant sheep, not as a means of beating them into submission. And note how the verse concludes: "but those who love them are diligent to discipline them." The differences between discipline and punishment are shown in the following chart:

DISCIPLINE VERSUS PUNISHMENT	
DISCIPLINE	**PUNISHMENT**
A climate of mutual respect.	Respect those in power.
Problems are opportunities.	Problems require punishment.
Preventive planning.	Reactive response.
Natural consequences.	Arbitrary consequences.
Reasons for standards.	"Do it because I said so."
Demand responsibility.	Demand obedience.
Teach caring values.	Teach rule compliance.
Adults as coaches.	Adults as rulers.

A Bar Mitzvah Gift

Richard Curwin, co-author of *Discipline with Dignity*, says that the most powerful lessons we teach youth come not from our words, but from the values communicated by our own behavior. He illustrates this idea with the following story about his own bar mitzvah gift to his son.

A bar mitzvah is a very special time for a Jewish boy. Two significant things happen. One is the trauma of having to read from the Torah in Hebrew in front of the whole congregation. It takes lots of courage and practice to do it right. The other significant thing is the receiving of many presents. Sometimes boys do so well that they get enough money to pay for college.

When my son, Andrew, was bar mitzvahed, I was having financial difficulties. I wanted to buy a memorable gift, but could not afford very much. When I asked Andrew what he wanted, he said, "A real California skateboard!" In fact, he wanted a Santa Cruz skateboard, the Cadillac of skateboards. I told him that I did not know if I could afford one, but I would check it out.

I found a newspaper ad that had skateboards on sale for $60. I decided that Andrew deserved to get one, and I would manage to pay that amount. When I told him, he was exuberant. We went down to the skateboard store together, but I was in for a big surprise. Though the ad had said $60, the skateboards were sold "à la carte." Everything besides the board was extra—even the wheels.

By the time they added everything up, the cost had escalated to $260! I knew I could no longer afford this present. When I looked at Andrew, who was trying to act composed, he said, "It's okay, Dad; I didn't want one anyway." I was so moved that he had responded that way, and I said, "If the government can do it, so can I! We'll take it," and nervously handed over my credit card, hoping it wouldn't max out.

On the way home, while Andrew was fiddling with the skateboard, he noticed the bill. "Dad, they made a mistake and only charged us $60!" I was so relieved that I said, "This is God's way of saying that you really deserve this skateboard."

But by the time I got home, I realized that this was not God speaking; it was stealing. I told Andrew that we owed $200 more, and asked him to call the store to tell them that we would bring the rest of the money in the next day.

Tears rolled down his face, and I asked him what was wrong. "Daddy, I was really glad that they only charged us $60 because I didn't want you to have to spend that much money on me when you don't have it. But if you didn't pay the full amount for it, I don't think I could have ever played with that skateboard because it wouldn't have been mine. I would have put it in the closet and never used it. I'm crying because I'm happy."

Reflecting later, I realized I would have paid far more than $260 to know my son had learned such a powerful lesson at his bar mitzvah![10]

Samuel Johnson once said, "Example is more efficacious than precept." No amount of preaching or moralizing can undo the lessons children learn by watching how we act. Even children who are chronically dishonest themselves hold adults to high standards. If we were to lie to a distrusting youth, it would be a long time before we would be forgiven for this dishonesty. Even the most deceitful children know what is right; they are just not doing it. But they will not change just by our preaching a principle. If a child is to change, it usually takes a person who consistently displays the principle in real life.

Principles and Pitfalls of Reparenting

When learning to fly a plane, the instructor prepares the student pilot for preventable disasters by teaching the student enough about the principles of flight to help prevent crashes. Keeping the following short checklist of important principles in mind will help you prevent crashes while you are reparenting challenging youth. To be forewarned is to be forearmed.

Principle 1. Children must be convinced that you can be trusted before they will invest.

Do not be too surprised when young people try to sabotage a relationship just when it seems things are beginning to go well. This often means they are getting ready to invest deeply in the relationship, but are afraid of being hurt again. Important authority figures have hurt them too many times in the past. They first want to make sure they can trust you before they commit too much, as was the case with Tami.

After a week-long canoeing trip, Tami had had enough. "Let me out of the car. I'm walking home! I hate you. I hate all of you, and I never want to see you again!" As Tami slammed the car door, she added, "I hope you die!"

The trip had been such a success. It was the first time we had seen real progress in Tami. She was beginning to open up to the youth leaders, who had been investing in her for so long. Yet now it seemed she was distancing herself more than ever.

Afraid of the relationships she was forming with these caring adults, Tami was attempting to squash those relationships before they could hurt her, something she had grown all too accustomed to doing.

Refusing to give up on Tami, these adults recognized her actions for what they were: a response to the fear of rejection and not a personal attack against them. Eventually, they won her trust, and Tami began making great strides.

Principle 2. As you assume the parenting role, you may be treated like others before you.

Youth will often transfer their feelings of anger or disappointment of others who have hurt them onto any new person who begins to fill that empty place in their lives. While they may know intuitively how important you are, their fear of being hurt again makes them leery of such a relationship. Scott Larson relates the following reparenting experience in which this happened:

> We had known Josh for 5 years while he was in a juvenile institution and had become very close during that time. But when he moved into our aftercare home, the relationship changed almost overnight. Instead of appreciating me for the increased commitment made, he seemed to hate me for it.
>
> Eventually, I confronted him about it: "Have I done something to offend you, Josh? We used to be very close, but now you seem to have all this anger toward me. What have I done?"

"You haven't done anything bad to me," he replied. "I think it's just the role you play. I see you like a father. And that role brings up a lot of anger in me. On one hand, I want to be close to you, but every time you say something to me, I get real mad. I just can't help my feelings. And you're the only one here I feel that way about. I think you're just in a role where you can't win."

That first year with Josh was miserable. We had to sit down and debrief many difficult situations, but slowly the father-role has been rebuilt in his life. And the way he responds to me is completely different than it used to be.

Principle 3. You must honor commitments even when children do not honor theirs.

We are held to a higher standard. As delinquency expert Denis Stott puts it, "We must be loyal to those who are disloyal, constant to the unreliable, forbearing to the provocative, always remembering that the greater the hate, the greater the need for love."[11] Just the time you are ready to give up on a child may be the time he or she decides you are worthy of trust.

Jim agreed to mentor 15-year-old Alex. The experience was not what he had envisioned. It was not that they did not connect. It was more that they did not even meet! Every time Jim went to Alex's house to pick him up as they had agreed, Alex was not home. This happened seven times in a row. The next time Jim was driving to Alex's, he had already decided that this was the last chance he was giving this relationship. It seemed more than obvious that Alex just was not interested. After ringing the doorbell several times, Jim walked back to his car, knowing he would not come back here again.

Just as he was about to drive away, Alex yelled out of a bedroom window, "Wait!" and came running out to the car. That day, the two of them began a friendship that would last several years. Jim later learned that Alex had been watching him from his window each time he came. He was testing Jim's commitment before he was going to invest in the relationship. In Jim's case, *showing up* was *more* than half the battle.

Every time you make commitments to children and keep them, even when they break theirs, you make major strides toward rebuilding the image of a positive authority figure. Why? Because the role you play as a significant, caring adult represents all the other adults who may have failed in that role with them over the years.

And although a series of failed relationships may contribute to a young person's distrust toward adults who "get too close," experiencing a successful relationship with an adult who keeps commitments can begin to reverse that distrust.

We tell our volunteer mentors, "You have to expect to phone kids 10 times to reach them once. Do not view this as wasted time. On the contrary, your persistence often works to strengthen the relationship like nothing else you can do."

Principle 4: Some youths trigger negative reactions that you must overcome.

As a chaplain in a large juvenile facility, Dan meets hundreds of new young people in a year. He cannot possibly be a surrogate father to all of them, but there are a few he feels called to "father." Over the years, Dan has "spiritually adopted," as he terms it, six different boys. He takes this quite seriously, maintaining a close bond with them long after they leave his institution.

Seventeen-year-old Matt had been in and out of custody several times by the time he came to Dan's office with a heavy heart. He told Dan that all he had ever really wanted in life was a dad, but that he had never had one. Dan tried to comfort him with words about God being a "Father to the fatherless" and the promise that "Even though our mother or father may forsake us, God will never forsake us." Matt left his office feeling as dejected as when he came.

Dan could not shake Matt's words and the possibility that God might be wanting him to spiritually adopt Matt as his seventh son. Why was he feeling so hesitant? In over a decade as a chaplain, Dan had never had a problem loving and accepting any child, regardless of his crime. But Matt was locked up for his involvement with friends in ritualistic satanic activities in which they had killed animals to drink their blood. Just the thought of such crimes totally repulsed Dan.

Though Dan had helped Matt break with his past satanic involvement, making him a *son* was something else. Then Dan thought of the hypocrisy of continuing to judge Matt for his sins because Dan had been forgiven for his own repulsive sins. More out of a sense of obedience to God than desire, Dan called Matt into his office.

"Matt, you told me you need a dad. Well, I've thought about it a great deal, and I'd like you to be my son. Not legally, as in the courts, but in a spiritual sense. It's something I take seriously. It's a commitment I would make for a lifetime. Please take some time to think about it, and we can talk about it again in a few days."

A few days later, Matt asked to speak with Dan privately. With tears in his eyes, Matt said, "I feel like God is answering all my prayers. I'd really like it if you would be my dad, Dan." In time, Dan developed deep feelings for his seventh son, but not until he took that first step of being willing to make a commitment to Matt.

Reparenting a child does not have to be as formal as Dan's "adoption." But one thing is certain; you can only fulfill that level of commitment in the lives of a few. Dan is attempting it with seven, but you only need to start with one. Perhaps that may require unlearning some prejudice, whether it is about a child's background or crime, race, or the way a child looks, acts, or talks.

We must be willing to admit our prejudices and grow beyond them. The child who might cause us to reel at the thought of reparenting may just be the one who needs us the most.

Principle 5: Conflicts can ruin relationships or they can build trust.

None of us likes to invest in a relationship that seems to be constantly in turmoil or conflict. But conflict, when properly resolved, does more than almost anything else to build a positive relationship. In fact, it is usually during this period in a relationship that youth discern whether we are really committed to them or not.

Most troubled youths have had few positive experiences with resolving conflict, and they see storms as signs that the relationship is about to be destroyed. In the past, conflicts only led to violence or rejection. Young people need to see that you will not walk away when things get tough.

The way you manage conflicts can expose youth to an entirely new model for resolving conflict. Sometimes you will need to be honest with children when you feel frustrated about their irresponsibility and apparent lack of commitment. Appropriately expressing your frustrations lets them know that this relationship is important to you. At other times, you may have inadvertently contributed to the conflict. Admitting this is also an excellent opportunity for growth and will earn you new respect.

Scott recalls one experience resolving conflict:

> One night, a weekly "house meeting" at one of our aftercare homes lasted nearly 4 hours. It was not a pleasant experience, for many difficult issues were raised. We wondered if Mike would choose to stay at the home, for most of the problems centered around him. At first he denied that he had sneaked out after curfew the previous night. But as evidence mounted against him, he tried blaming others, reacting in explosive anger. Finally, he broke down and admitted his guilt.
>
> When we were about to disband, Mike remarked, "This was great. We need to have these kind of meetings more often!" How could he be so encouraged about such a difficult meeting? He had experienced having the dark

side of himself confronted and exposed, while still being loved. He could see that we were committed to working the issues all the way through, not just giving up. That gave him a tremendous amount of security. He no longer needed to carry the weight of his guilt. It was finally out in the open where he could own it and receive help in changing his actions.

A Blueprint for Building Relationship Beachheads

In his book, *At Risk: Bringing Hope to Hurting Teenagers*, Scott Larson shares a four-step blueprint for building relationships with difficult youth:

1. Realize that you must be the one to start the relationship. Youth will not do it. You may even need to start it several times before it begins to gel. Often they will not even take your invitation to get together seriously, because they cannot really believe that you want to get to know them. But seldom will a young person turn down a sincere adult who really wants to get together with them. They may be a bit apprehensive and nervous, but they will also be shocked that you actually *want* to spend time with them.

2. Plan your time together around an activity. It can be very intimidating for both you and the youth just to get together "to talk," especially when you both realize after about 5 minutes that you have run out of things to talk about. It quickly becomes clear that you do not have much in common, as you each wonder, *Now what do we do?*

It is much better if you can organize your time around an activity such as attending a sports event, biking, going to a movie, or eating out at a restaurant. Doing activities together also gives you the opportunity to create memories you can talk about in the future. Adults are generally more open to doing a specific task like coaching, tutoring, or job training than just hanging out, "bonding" with a child. But significant relationships are the byproducts of doing activities together.

3. Try to schedule some activities just for the two of you, away from the child's friends. Youth act differently when they are with their friends because they have an image to maintain. Never force them to choose between you and their friends—you will lose every time. When they are away from their friends, they can afford to be more themselves.

4. Do not be afraid to meet them on their turf. Doing so always gives you something to talk about. You may know nothing about what life is like where they live, so ask them. Suddenly, they are the experts, not you. Your being humble enough to be the student also makes them much more willing to listen to you when you share things that you may know more about than they do.[12]

Reparenting is certainly not easy. But those who dare to invest at such a level will find that not only will the lives of hurting youth be changed, but their own lives will be changed as well.

CHAPTER 8

Redirecting

cultivating competence

The crowning achievement of education is to reach the child's heart and to convince him of our fervent love, at the very moment when we are pointing out mistakes.
—Johann Pestalozzi, Swiss educational reformer
(1746–1827)

A CENTURY AGO, pioneer youth workers in many nations set out on a mission to cultivate positive strengths in even the most difficult children. They discovered that even the most recalcitrant youth could be changed, if provided opportunities for corrective guidance in environments that met their needs and tapped their hidden potential. A sampling of these pioneers includes persons from many nations:

- Father Flanagan founded Boys Town and Floyd Starr founded the Starr Commonwealth for wayward youth. Both were renowned for their belief that so-called bad children would be good if given opportunities for love, learning, work, and spiritual guidance.

- Maria Montessori worked with Italy's slum children. She contended that their God-given intelligence and highly absorbent minds were unknown in traditional schools, which "pinned them to their desks like rows of beautiful dead butterflies."

- Sylvia Ashton-Warner described her rebellious Maori students in New Zealand as "volcanoes with two vents—aggression and creativity." Preferring creativity, she threw out the colonial curriculum. As children wrote and illustrated their own books, once aggressive students became actively motivated learners.

The Pygmalion optimism shared by these great pioneers in youth work was perhaps best embodied by Karl Wilker, who in 1917 transformed Berlin's worst delinquency institution into a model of effective treatment. Wilker taught his coworkers that their job was to find the positive qualities of these youths no matter how deeply they were hidden. He demanded that staff respect even disrespectful children. And he fully expected that irresponsible youths could be taught responsibility for their behavior. But when Hitler came to power, Wilker's writings were burned, and he fled to South Africa where Alan Paton was beginning similar work with Black delinquents.

Strength Building

Alan Paton is best known as the novelist who wrote *Cry the Beloved Country*, but his first vocation was reeducating outcast youth of the apartheid underclass. Paton challenged the notion that placing delinquents in punitive programs of hardness, austerity, and deprivation would teach them that crime does not pay.

Like Wilker, Paton transformed a large locked institution into a model of positive intervention. He also advocated for serving most troubled youth in their own homes whenever possible. He saw the solution to delinquency as transforming their problems into positive strengths:

> A child is often delinquent because he has been deprived of fundamental needs of security, affection, and outlets for his creative and emotional impulses. The change

in him is remarkable when these deep needs are satisfied. His insolence, secretiveness, untimely independence, and disobedience disappear when he lives in the kind of community in which he finds a meaning for his own life. It is quite wrong to suppose that these opportunities are evidences of pampering and sentimental benevolence. They are designed to restore self-reliance, self-respect and self-trust.[1]

The optimism of these early pioneers was lost in the second half of the twentieth century. Youth work became professionalized and compartmentalized in bureaucratic systems of education, mental health, social service, and justice. The focus changed from building strengths and relationships to treating pathology and controlling behavior. While arguments raged over rehabilitation versus punishment, both approaches were reactive and pessimistic. Isolated voices called for a return from deficit-based to strength-based approaches. Now, a century after the groundbreaking work of youth pioneers, we are finally experiencing a paradigm shift toward positive youth development.

"Why do kids go right?"

We have been created with remarkable capacities to overcome problems; to survive, thrive, and learn. The theme of overcoming adversity is prominent throughout the scriptures, as is portrayed in the story of the prodigal son. In fact, struggle and hardship often become the very foundation for character and faith development.

Conflict and its resolution are also universal themes in secular literature. In *A Farewell to Arms*, Hemingway writes, "Life breaks everybody, but some become strong at the broken places." More recently, the behavioral sciences have validated this age-old wisdom as well. The movement toward "strength-building" approaches with youth has been sparked by researchers who study human resilience. They began to ask "Why do kids go right?" instead of "Why do they go wrong?"

In 1955, Emmy Werner and Ruth Smith began a longitudinal study of 700 high-risk children born on the Hawaiian island of Kauai. They were born with multiple difficulties—premature birth, low birth weight, poverty, broken families, parental alcoholism, and parental mental illnesses. Not surprisingly, most of these children were getting into trouble by the time they were adolescents. But about 60% of those with high-risk behavior were able to turn their lives around by age 30. Their success was not accidental, but was facilitated by such factors as encouragement from mentors and a grounding in spiritual faith.[2]

Many of the leaders in the study of resilience are survivors who beat the odds to overcome their own abysmal childhoods. Warren Rhodes was a gang-involved, delinquent youth who went on to chair the psychology department at Morgan State University. He and Kim Hoey wrote *Overcoming Childhood Misfortune: Children Who Beat the Odds,* a book that chronicles eight successful adults who overcame troubled backgrounds.

Beyond their personal resourcefulness, important environmental supports nurtured their resilience. Religious instruction, a supportive relationship with a caring adult, structure and discipline, and opportunities to develop skills were reported by those who survived the journey from troubled youth to successful adult.

Brenda Jarmon was a high school dropout who had had two children by age 16, and had spent 3 years working in a chicken processing plant by age 18. She turned her life around and is now a social work professor at Florida State University.

Providing national leadership to prevent parenthood among children, Professor Jarmon is highly respected among students who say "She knows whereof she speaks." She sees the key to building resilience in enhancing young people's problem-solving and decision-making skills by having them address the real-life consequences of their actions.

On first examination, cases like these would have offered little reason for optimism. Their records were filled with reports of failed interventions. They had rejected relationships and had been labeled conduct disordered, affectionless, and unattached. They did not learn from their mistakes and continued to get into more and more trouble.

When children such as these come to court, prosecutors tend to look only at their history of failure and argue that the youth have failed to take advantage of opportunities for rehabilitation. Yet Rhodes and Jarmon not only survived but went on to become professionals in the field of youth work. What made the difference?

John Seita was able to overcome his own turbulent background of growing up in foster care and youth institutions. He highlights four crucial resilience factors that were present for Rhodes and Jarmon as well:

1. Connectedness. "Tenaciously caring adults did not give up although I tried to torpedo the relationships." John also found connectedness spiritually: "People were not always there for me—or I would not allow them to be. Praying was a way to talk and reach out to God. He listened as I poured out my heart."

2. Continuity. From age 8 to 12, John was bounced through a dozen foster homes and institutions. "I was like a piece of tape that had been stuck to a surface and pulled up so many times it no longer could attach." It took many years before John finally found adults he could trust to remain in his life.

Faith in God also provides an important continuity. Even at times when others fail youths, a relationship with God can sustain hope, as was the case with John.

3. Dignity. Troubled youth are devalued and learn to devalue themselves. John describes rats running over his bed at night in a court shelter. He also recalls standing nude in lines of boys waiting for their clothing to be handed out. "If I've been abandoned to a place like this, what worth could I possibly have?" he reasoned. Although he was an angry, raging youth, he still encountered some adults who treated him with dignity, which allowed him to maintain a sense of worth in the midst of abandonment.

4. Opportunity. How did John transform from hating teachers to now holding a doctorate in education? "I was exposed to opportunities even if I didn't always take advantage of them—sports, education, and career options. Staff were on a talent hunt, finding my talents even before I knew they existed."[3]

Are these stories of resilience merely tales of rare "superkids" who scale high-risk childhoods to become superstar adults? Seita contends that all children have the potential to develop resilience, and he calls for communities to commit themselves to creating positive youth development for all children. This will demand more than just looking out for our own children. We will have to "raise the neighborhood," as Dr. Seita illustrates below:

> A father was being consoled at this son's funeral by friends and neighbors while his wife sobbed nearby. The son had been the victim of a drive by shooting; he was 16. "You were a good father," consoled one friend, while a second offered sympathetically, "Robert was a great kid, he was a good athlete, a good student, and I'll always remember our times together volunteering at the food bank. You had a great son, I'll miss him. I'm so sorry for you and Janice, you did everything right." The father slowly turned his red-rimmed eyes toward his long-time friend, "No," he replied, sadly shaking his head, "I didn't do everything right." He continued on as his startled friends listened, "I didn't raise the rest of the neighborhood."[4]

In the remainder of this chapter, we examine ways adults can attempt to raise the neighborhood by cultivating the strengths and competence of youth through providing connectedness, continuity, dignity, and opportunity. This is a major shift from the preoccupation with deviance and control, which has become the norm in dealing with youth at risk.

Strengthening the Conscience

John Gibbs, of Ohio State University, was a colleague of the leading moral development researcher, Lawrence Kohlberg of Harvard. Gibbs cites research showing that 9 of 10 delinquents embrace many positive values, even if their behavior does not show it.[5] Even mean-spirited youth who talk like they do not care for anybody are often putting on a front of toughness for self-protection.

Certainly, these youth may make many thinking errors, such as blaming others, being self-centered, assuming the worst, and minimizing and mislabeling their own problems. But anti-social thinking does not mean that a youth has no conscience. Gibbs concludes that thinking errors often cause youth to avoid feeling guilt for behavior that has hurt others.

The chart on page 124 will help you quickly assess a youth's stage of conscience development. Most adults function at the top two rungs of the ladder. But those who do not advance beyond the lower rungs of "power" or "deals" will not be responsible young people and, as adults, they will not be solid parents and citizens.

All children are very self-centered when they begin their lives, but by observing positive adults and peers in the normal course of events, most develop concern for others and internal behavior controls. Likewise, the lack of love or discipline and negative peer influence can arrest or distort conscience. Such youngsters often need conscience-development training, something best done in the context of caring relationships.

To create empathy and concern for others in youth with weak consciences or self-centered biases, a concentrated "dose" of opportunities may be needed to jump-start their conscience development.

THE LADDER OF CONSCIENCE DEVELOPMENT[6]

PRINCIPLES

"Just and caring."
Concerned for others, sticks to inner values even if challenged, feels appropriate guilt, and tries to redress wrongs.

COOPERATION

"Let's get along."
Generally treats others fairly and wants to please others. Is uncomfortable when violating rules, but can be misled by others.

DEALS

"What's in it for me?"
Superficial warmth but is self-centered, often needs external controls, and conforms to rules to keep from being caught.

POWER

"Might makes right."
Shows little empathy or concern about hurting others, lacks self-control, and shows little guilt even if hurting others.

The following successful approaches have been used to remedy problems of conscience development.

Strengthen Prosocial Adult Bonds

Because conscience develops through ties to caring adults and peers, strengthening these bonds can help foster positive moral development. Adults who match their roles to the needs of children will become more powerful figures in their lives. But healthy bonds are different at differing stages of a child's development, as shown below.

THE MATURING BONDS BETWEEN CHILDREN AND ADULTS

STAGE OF DEVELOPMENT	WHAT IS IMPORTANT?	THE ADULT'S ROLE
Infant/toddler	"my needs"	Satisfy needs
Preschool	"please adults"	Teach standards Provide approval
Elementary	"be fair"	Uphold authority Guide behavior
Middle school	"fit in" "be responsible"	Role model Group facilitator
High school	"do what's right" "care for others"	Counselor Advocate Confidant

—Adapted from material from Mary Wood, Development Therapy and Teaching Institute, Athens, Georgia.

Strengthen Prosocial Peer Bonds

Because youth with weak consciences tend to seek out friends who think like them, it is important to provide opportunities for friendships with prosocial peers who will not support delinquent values and thinking.

This may require transforming negative peer cultures. A number of promising programs have been developed for this purpose, including school bully-proofing programs, Natural Peer Helpers, Resolving Conflict Creatively Programs, Positive Peer Culture, and EQUIP treatment models.

In traditional programs with youth at risk, adults try to control youth or to get youth to accept the passive role of patients in need of a helping professional. Some programs today tap the power of young people to become partners in solving their own problems. These strength-based programs empower youth to help solve the problems of their peers in a climate of care and concern. Students can also become involved in self-governance. As youth are given opportunities to participate in setting the rules that govern their community, they also begin to gain a greater overall perspective. Among successful programs that involve youth in self-governance are youth courts, Just Community programs, and the Boys Town empowerment model.

Develop Moral Decision-Making Skills

Boys Town research on at-risk youth indicates that social-skill instruction can help foster moral development. For example, a youth who lacks skills in managing anger or accepting criticism makes many bad choices in relationships with others. Having gained skills in these areas, the youth now has a real moral choice because he or she understands the tangible alternatives to becoming angry and hurting others.

The EQUIP model developed by John Gibbs and colleagues uses peer-group discussion to challenge moral thinking. This is not just warmed-over "values clarification," where youth decide what they think is right. Rather, adults guide this process by posing real-life dilemmas that have a moral answer. Typical scenarios involve temptations to use drugs or to engage in sexual or delinquent behavior. Because different levels of moral development are present in a typical group, youths must justify their moral thinking in the face of challenges from more advanced peers and adult leaders.

Provide Character Education and Religious Training

A leader in the revival of character education in schools is Tom Lickona, who has developed curricula to teach how self-indulgent behavior damages human relationships. Writing about the neglected heart, he helps youth reflect on the hurtful effects of sexual involvement outside of the marriage bond.[7] A wide variety of curricula for character education are now available for use in both secular and faith-based settings.

Studies have shown that youth who have been involved in religious education are further ahead in moral development, self-control, and respect for others. Psychologist Merton Strommen found that the message of a loving God fostered concern for others and decreased bigotry and prejudice.[8] But he also found that religious training that centers around an angry God can actually increase prejudice.

Some traditional methods of religious education can turn youths off. However, in our work with delinquents, we have found that Bible studies led by consistent, relational adults who are positive rather than condemning draw about 40% of the population and offer a powerful transforming force in young lives.

From Hurting to Helping

"Blessed are the weak" is one of the Beatitudes in the Bible. But exploiting the weak has become the norm in our power-oriented culture. Likewise, many troubled youth use their power to hurt or exploit others. Some were themselves violated by adults or older siblings. Others learned the lessons of power on the streets, from school bullies, and in the media. Because power is the bottom rung of the ladder of moral development, a priority must be to help young people move from power to principles in relationships with others.

We will now consider four important ways that help young people learn to move from hurting to helping: putting bullies out of business, confronting "lookism," healing racism, and fostering altruism.

Putting Bullies Out of Business

Research shows that bullying is a much more serious problem in U.S. schools than in most other nations. Most adults can recall painful experiences at the hand of school bullies. Until recently, such behavior was tolerated with a rationalization that "kids will be kids." But a wealth of research from Scandinavia shows that much school bullying can be prevented with a three-pronged approach targeted at the bully, the victim, and the silent majority.

Because bullies are at great risk for criminal behavior as adults and abuse of their own children, programs that target school bullying are powerful prevention strategies.

Bullies must be confronted about the serious thinking errors that they use to rationalize their abuse of others. For example, a statement like, "We were just teaching that sissy to act like a man," needs to be challenged by demonstrating how strength lies in the restraint of power, not abuse of it.

We must also recognize that many bullies are, in fact, effective leaders of at least some peers, albeit negative leaders. They need positive opportunities to exercise leadership. Norwegian schools have been effective at putting former bullies in the role of being big buddies to new children who enter their classes.

Not only must the perpetrators of bullying be confronted, but the victims also need help in becoming more assertive and in believing they are worthy enough not to deserve the status of victim. Youths who act like victims usually remain victims. Believing they somehow deserve such treatment, they see very few options and possess little motivation to change.

But bullies can survive only when the silent majority lets them act with impunity. In a school, youth group, or family, we must build an ethos that says nobody hurts another person here. Adults must be scrupulous role models if this value is to be believed. Speaking up to stop bullying is not tattling, but an act of maturity and courage.

Not only do youth need to be trained to stand up for those who are picked on in their schools, they must also be challenged with the incredible task of reaching out to and befriending their peers who are being ostracized. Every teen is aware of those who sit in school cafeterias and walk down hallways, continually bearing the brunt of others' tactics of intimidation. Youth must recognize how their merely standing by silently, observing such antics, is just as bad as participating in them.

Confronting "Lookism"

While bullying is particularly common among boys, among girls the process of *lookism* is equally destructive. Polly Nichols defines lookism as ranking persons by superficial physical appearances.[9] Though more subtle than sexism or racism, lookism is also a more pervasive thinking error. The great majority of young people report being dissatisfied with how they look. From early adolescence, they are preoccupied with physical appearance in themselves and peers. When grave importance is attached to random human differences, superficial traits become the measure of the worth of self and others. Lookism is both commonplace and extremely hurtful. Sadker and Sadker relate this incident:

> The auditorium was packed with more than a thousand students who were restless as they listened to announcements. A heavy, awkward tenth grader made her way across the stage to reach the microphone. As she walked, several male students made loud barking noises to signify she was a dog. Others oinked like pigs. Later, a slender long-haired senior walked to the mike; she was greeted by catcalls and whistles. Nobody attempted to stop the demeaning and hurtful public evaluation of the appearance of these teenage girls.[10]

Obviously, if the students had hurled epithets about race or disability, adults would have held them accountable. But under the excuse that "boys will be boys," a massive amount of sexual harassment occurs. Equally tragic, young people begin to evaluate themselves against these thinking errors. If they fail to measure up, they become mired in self-hatred. This is pervasive in girls, but many boys are equally subject to ridicule and shame because of a perceived lack of macho traits.

Healing Racism

"What do you expect us to do?" complained one young man in a detention center. "Because we're Puerto Rican people won't hire us. Believe me, I've tried. But you got to be white to get a job where I live. We got to make money some way if we're going to survive. What would you do?"

Sadly, he makes a very good point. In the Larsons' aftercare home, we have witnessed too many instances where a minority youth asks an employer if they are hiring. The answer is often "No," though they may be standing directly under a "Help Wanted" sign. In some of the cases, a white boy from the same Larson home would then ask the same question, to which he is told, "Yes, we're hiring for several shifts. Would you like to fill out an application?"

Prejudicial thinking is one of the most pervasive sicknesses in our culture today. John Woodall of the Harvard Medical School describes it as a "disease of the mind," where persons who are weak project their inadequacies onto others. This pattern is particularly destructive in our power-based, materialistic culture. Prejudice infects both those who act as if they are superior to others and those who are the victims of the prejudice.

The late Spencer Perkins, son of community development pioneer John Perkins, grew up in Mississippi where, as a young man, his father had been beaten bloody by racist law officers. Even after Spencer, an African American, had moved north into a white neighborhood, he would often hear car doors lock when he came near. But rather than staying bitter, he reached out to really get to know his Anglo brothers and sisters. As a result, he and Chris Rice became best friends, co-authored the book *More Than Equals,* and began leading seminars nationwide on racial reconciliation.

Ranking persons based on racial, ethnic, or gender differences is rampant in the general population, and persons in faith communities are not immune. In most communities, Sunday morning is still the most segregated time of the week. Nathan Rutstein has been studying racism since the days when he was a young journalist assigned to cover Martin Luther King's civil rights campaigns. He concludes that decades of attempts at integration have failed to recognize that racism is a virulent spiritual and mental disease, which is unlikely to be remedied by laws, multicultural activities, or "tolerance training." We need more than polite toleration of one another. Instead, we must recognize the spiritual principle of the oneness of all humans as children created in the image of God.[11]

In cooperation with churches, schools, police, and other community groups, Rutstein has established hundreds of Institutes for Healing Racism. Beginning with participation in two-day Healing Racism Institutes, persons of diverse backgrounds come together in an environment of trust to learn how the irrational ideas underlying racism have developed and how racism has affected their lives. They then begin the difficult work of eradicating racism from their communities. Rutstein contends that multiculturalism as currently taught may have fostered superficial friendliness but has not made us friends with persons from differing racial and cultural backgrounds.

Fostering Altruism

Some troubled youth disparage the value of giving of themselves to others and instead embrace lifestyles of selfishness and the exploitation of others. But most still have some flickering concern for others. They may, for example, steal a woman's purse in the subway and then give 10 dollars of it to a homeless person as they are counting the money.

It is difficult to "feel for" persons who are not like us in age, culture, or race. But ethical behavior involves reaching out to befriend even the stranger. If we want to foster generosity in youth, we must help them reach beyond their self-serving circle of friends. This involves direct involvement in volunteer activities where young persons have real-life opportunities to help another human in need.

The most powerful experiences to develop empathy and perspective come from examining how our own behavior has victimized others. After his first time feeding the homeless in Boston, a boy in one of Straight Ahead Ministries' aftercare homes remarked, "I used to kick or steal from those people when they were sleeping in the park. But tonight I got to feed them. It made me feel ashamed for how I used to be. I'm just glad I have a chance to pay them back in some way."

Structured victim-offender programs also encourage youth to see how their actions have hurt another person. A dramatic example is a program operated by a church agency in Germany for youth who have been involved in Neo-Nazi gangs, which commit hate crimes against Jews and other ethnic groups.

These youth are taken on a 3-week experiential learning project to Auschwitz in Poland where they work rebuilding monuments to the victims of the death camps. They also interview elderly people who had direct experiences with the camps in their childhood. They come face to face with the Holocaust in the stories shared by kindly, venerable survivors. Empathy becomes the ultimate weapon in fighting the prejudicial attitudes and beliefs that lead to crimes of hate.

Correcting Thinking Errors

Redl and Wineman in their classic book, *Children Who Hate*, were among the first to describe how troubled children use "cognitive distortions," or thinking errors, that interfere with accurately interpreting the behavior of self or others.[12] For example, a bully might justify an attack on a victim in this way: "Well, he looked at me funny, so he deserved to get hit." Unless these thinking errors are remedied, the bully will never feel remorse or be motivated to change such behavior.

One exciting accomplishment in work with youth has been the development of programs to identify and correct thinking distortions common in youth at risk. These programs have been successful with delinquents, with emotionally disturbed children, and with any youth showing distorted or prejudicial thinking. Biased thinking drives much negative behavior, and adults need skills if they are to help the youth think more clearly. There are four primary types of thinking errors that can be remedied.[13]

1. Self-Centered Thinking

Self-centered thinking occurs when a youth considers only his or her own views, needs, feelings, and rights. This core problem of self-centeredness has always been at the crux of strained relationships. According to professor John Gibbs, this is the "generic" thinking error, and all others are simply more specific subsets of a thinking pattern that considers self at the detriment of others. Some common examples might be:

I took it because I needed it.

If I cheat on my boyfriend, it's nobody's business but my own.

I don't care what happens to other people. I just watch out for number one.

The goal in remediating these errors is to increase opportunities for youths to listen to the thoughts and to feel the feelings of others. Because self-centered thinking may be very entrenched, repeated experiences of connecting with others are more likely to change the thinking than will preaching. Instead of getting into an argument, it is sometimes best just to ask a question that might create a bit of dissonance in the youth's mind, such as "I wonder what would happen if everybody thought that way?" Service activities that cultivate generosity are excellent means of countering self-centered thinking.

2. Minimizing or Mislabeling

The thinking error of minimizing or mislabeling occurs when a youth depicts harmful behavior as being harmless or even clever. This includes referring to others with dehumanizing labels. For example:

I just roughed him up a little.

Getting drunk or wasted is fun.

She deserved to get raped because of the way she dresses.

One effective response is to "relabel" the problem for the young person. If a theft is described with such words as "strong," "macho," or "slick," the adult can reframe these labels as "immature" or "sneaky." One must be careful to attach labels *only* to the behavior, however, and never to the person. The message that must come through is: "This is a very immature way of acting for someone with your talents." By pairing positive statements that recognize the dignity of the person with statements that confront the person's behavior and thinking errors, we communicate powerfully without inciting resistance.

3. Assuming the Worst

Common in distrustful youth is a pessimistic bias about the intentions of others. Many youth also assume the worst about their own abilities. In addition, they may be preoccupied with all the possible negative events that can befall them. Some common examples might include:

I can't help it if I lose my temper a lot.

I hate school because everything they teach is boring.

People pretend they are your friends but will just stab you in the back.

Children as young as 4 have shown such pessimistic biases in thinking. For example, the child who has not learned to trust adults may go to school assuming he or she will not like the teacher. Because thinking errors are reasonably accurate private logic, given the way the child has experienced life, it often takes new experiences, as well as verbal discussions, to reframe his or her thinking.

4. Blaming Others

Attributing blame for one's own actions or shortcomings to some outside source is another thinking error. Such children see themselves as the pawns or victims of others. Common statements might be:

> If he leaves his wallet lying around, he deserves to have it stolen.
>
> People make me mad so I lose my temper.
>
> My parents don't care about me, so why should I care?

Youths who act like victims and will not take responsibility for their own actions have little motivation to change. Sometimes this thinking is designed to avoid painful truths about ourselves. The goal is not to convert blaming others into self-blame, but to help youths take responsibility for their behavior. The issue of responsibility is of critical importance and will be discussed further in the next chapter.

Confronting With Respect

Thinking error programs have become very popular as a "treatment veneer" in some correctional programs that otherwise ignore the needs of youth. Just to tell young people that they are using "criminal thinking" or to make them engage in superficial activities like reading lists of thinking errors is far less powerful than genuine communication.

In our experience, errors in thinking are often best corrected in a peer-group situation where a youth can compare his or her views with those of others and be challenged by them. For example, one youth in a positive peer culture group was bragging about "deflowering chicks." This is a mislabeling error that distorts truth and prevents youths from facing the consequences of their behavior. His group challenged him by asking, "What would you do if somebody treated your sister like that?" He was immediately sobered as he reflected on the contradiction that he would protect his sister against the likes of himself.

People have been rationalizing immoral behavior since the beginning of time. Simply reciting the Ten Commandments will not change lives. Thinking errors cannot be considered separately from a person's feelings, values, and spiritual beliefs, for these are the things that influence one's thoughts.

While adults must not be afraid to confront a young person about thinking errors, such confrontation must be done in a respectful manner that preserves his or her dignity. It is also helpful to remember that each of us is also capable of slipping into these same faulty patterns of thinking.

Connecting to Youths in Conflict

Rebellious and resistant youth fight with or flee from adults. They distrust all authority, getting locked into conflict cycles. Because they refuse to listen to or learn from adults, they fail to gain the skills for successful living. Trying in their own way to cope with a hostile world, they are likely to engage in chronic patterns of self-defeating behavior. But it is the youth who avoid or attack adults who are most in need of guidance and discipline.

We need new strategies for disengaging from destructive cycles if we are to help young people examine their behavior and learn more effective ways of coping with the world. Motivating them to learn and change requires the skills of a coach, one who can draw out their inner strengths and talents.

"Our eyes seldom met."

One of the things that makes connecting with any young person difficult is that they often appear very intimidating to their elders. Our entire culture seems to revolve around youth. They are the ones who know and embody what's in style in terms of clothing, music, and vocabulary. We adults are seen as "old-fashioned" and "out of touch."

These apprehensions only intensify when it comes to at-risk kids. Most of us understand very little of what life is like for them. And because of their myriad of trust issues, they are just as leery about getting to know us. Though historically the lives of children and adults were closely intertwined, ours may be the first culture in the history of the world where grown-ups and youth try hard to avoid one another.

Youth researcher Peter Benson once told 300 senior citizens in Bemidji, Minnesota, that 80% of adults avert their eyes when meeting a youth of middle school age. These elders resolved to go into the streets of their city and purposely smile at every youth they encountered. In a few weeks, youth were complaining that something strange was happening: "All the old people are laughing at us."[14] While their intentions were good, a smile from somebody who hurries away is superficial and suspect.

Laypersons are not the only ones who avoid youth. In his autobiographical book about his experience as a delinquent youth, Waln Brown retrieved from his case files scores of diagnostic reports written by professionals who had worked with him. They submitted complex assessments about his problems, but most never really understood him. "Our eyes seldom met," recalled Waln.[15] It is easier to diagnose difficult children as having attachment disorders than to seriously attempt to attach to them.

The nineteenth-century Italian youth pastor Father Don Bosco challenged his staff to engage troubled youth; to have fun with them; and by living in close contact, to become central forces in their lives. In his later years, Bosco lamented that the young priests had disengaged themselves from direct contact, finding any excuse to talk with one another rather than with youth. In turn, youth would be found furtively whispering among one another, and the climate of his school became one of youth against adults.

In our visits to programs for troubled teens around the world, we have found that one useful strategy for taking the pulse of a program's effectiveness is to note the percentage of staff members who are in direct contact with youth. In one facility we visited recently, only 1 in 13 was communicating with teens. The rest either stood with their arms crossed along the perimeter, assuming the role of jailer, or had retreated into offices to busy themselves with paperwork. As our colleague, the late Al Trieschman, often said, "In some places it might be better to put the kids in the file cabinets so they could get more care." Only adults who actively engage youth will become significant forces in their lives.

Making Small Connections: *Carpe Minutum*

The 1989 movie *Dead Poets Society* popularized the Latin phrase *carpe diem,* which means "seize the day." We propose that busy adults at least commit themselves to *carpe minutum,* or "seize the minute." Many adults say they do not have enough time for their own children, let alone someone else's. Even so, we can all do many small things. For practice, choose a child you occasionally see (or look away from) in passing and try to make small connections. A smile is at least a start.

Larry Brendtro relates this *carpe minutum* experience:

> While visiting a middle school church camp where two of our children were counselors, I met a tall, thin boy clad in paramilitary garb. He had a record of delinquent behavior, and it was obvious he had made few friends during the week. Because no other camper stood near him at the closing campfire, I joined the circle at his side.
>
> "Hi, I'm Larry. What's your name?" He peered from under the brim of his army hat and shyly said, "Martin." *Bingo!* I thought. "Oh, I have a brother named Martin," I added. This was a conversation stopper. Grasping at what to say next, I settled on "Boy, I'm chilly tonight. I wish I had dressed like you. Where do you get those?" He beamed as if he had suddenly been promoted to expert status on military attire.
>
> After small talk, we joined the others in songs. Then, as a benediction, all campers were invited to "share the

peace." This is a nice, but sometimes awkward, ritual where you never are quite certain of whether to shake hands or give a hug. But hugging was in vogue on the last night of camp. However, most of the hugs offered to Martin were not from peers but from staff trying to be nice. Even then, Martin was very selective on the hugs he would reciprocate. Because he turned several offers into stiff handshakes, I was surprised when my turn came to be greeted, I received a hug worthy of a warrior.

Of course, this fleeting encounter will likely have little lasting significance for Martin, except it may have softened some of the rejection he might have felt on his last night at camp. It also illustrates how we often push away the youth who need us the most. Small kindnesses are the building blocks of relationships. And for the starving, even a tiny treat is a feast.

Hunting for Hidden Talent

John Seita was a troubled teen who never knew his father, and his mother was an alcoholic and prostitute. He was removed from her custody at age 8. Over the next 4 years, John would fail in a dozen court-ordered foster homes and juvenile institutions. He bonded to nobody and constantly ran away to return to the streets. John never did get a family and spent his entire adolescence in residential placements.

Like most youth with long histories of failed attachments, John hated any adult who tried to be an authority in his life. Only by decoding John's behavior can we understand what his rejection of others meant: "I say I hate you because I know you won't love me." Rebuilding such deeply damaged children takes time. In John's case, healing began at age 12 when he finally found a stable residential placement. But it would take a dozen more years of progress with setbacks before he could begin to show his real potential.

Spending his teen years at Starr Commonwealth, a Michigan facility for troubled youth, for the first time John started to connect with several adults in surrogate parenting relationships. He began to find continuity in this extended placement, and he carried several reparenting relationships into young adulthood, including Starr's chaplain.

John experienced dignity from adults, even when he did not reciprocate respect, and his hidden talents were cultivated in school, sports, and interpersonal relationships. John finished high school while residing in a community group home. He started college, but for several years experienced recurrent academic challenges and difficulties keeping his first jobs. At times, his development was slowed by the speed bumps of life failures, but the important thing was that he was now trying to learn from his mistakes.

While we all would like quick turnarounds in the lives of our youth, those whose serious problems have been festering for years will demand our patience. John's life was a disaster for his first 12 years, so it is not surprising that it took a dozen more for him to settle down. In time, John graduated from college, went to graduate school, and completed his doctorate at Western Michigan University. He has worked with a major youth foundation and is an expert on youth development. In a book he coauthored on his life, Seita describes how to connect to highly guarded youth like himself. The chart on page 143 presents his recommendations for connecting with troubled youth.

Because we tend to focus so much on negative behavior with troubled youth, it should not surprise us when the results of our efforts are less than exhilarating. Positive outcomes are seldom achieved by focusing on the negative. But when a young person's positive attributes are recognized, encouraged, and praised, real change for the better is just around the corner. That is what redirecting is all about. Before we can expect young people to redirect their energies, we must be willing to redirect ours.

RECLAIMING UNRECLAIMABLE KIDS

1. **Recast all problems as learning opportunities.** *Please coach me, don't scold me.*

2. **Become a talent scout.** *Help me find success, and you become important to me.*

3. **Provide fail-safe relationships.** *I need to know that you won't give up on me.*

4. **Increase dosages of nurturing.** *A person like me really needs a fan club.*

5. **Don't crowd.** *When you get too close, I will need to back away for a while.*

6. **Decode the meaning of behavior.** *I often try to hide what I really think.*

7. **Be authoritative, not authoritarian.** *Help me learn how to control myself.*

8. **Respect the disrespectful.** *I don't deserve your respect but desperately need it.*

9. **Make me a partner in my healing.** *I am the only real expert on my life.*

10. **Touch in small ways.** *I watch you and notice the little things you say and do.*

11. **Give seeds time to grow.** *Please be patient with me— I'm still learning.*

12. **Connect youth to cultural and spiritual roots.** *I need to know there is a purpose for my life.*

—From a forthcoming book by John Seita and Larry Brendtro.

CHAPTER 9

Reconciling
cultivating responsibility

Talking together and an attitude of forgiveness towards even the worst offenders seemed to us the most valuable method.

—August Aichorn, Austrian psychologist (1878–1949)

IN EARLIER TIMES, a simple system was employed to make children behave. The same procedures were used on both children and domestic animals, namely obedience training through punishment and occasional rewards. Usually a stern warning from adults would suffice. If unheeded, the warning would be followed by swift physical pain. Some still contend that if we would just "take off the gloves" and revert to earlier practices, we would be able to raise disciplined and respectful children.

Scaring Children Straight?

Perhaps the most famous book on disciplining children is *Der Struwwelpeter*, written in 1854 by a leading German physician, Heinrich Hoffman. Translated into all major European languages, it was used for a half century by parents who did not know what to do with wild children. Basically, it is a picture storybook to be read to small children, showing them the terrible things that happen when children do not obey elders.

Hoffman wanted an alternative to hitting children. Because most cultures use stories to pass on values to children, he reasoned that a storybook might teach them to be obedient. His plan was to scare children when they were little so they would not have to be hit when they were big.

Each story in *Der Struwwelpeter* is about a different problem child—the bully, the bigot, the hyperactive, the oppositional, and several more. The accompanying illustrations capture the general idea. Girls who disobey and play with matches are cremated (see below). Boys who suck their thumbs have them amputated.

Hoffman's baby book sold millions of copies and gave bad dreams to generations of youngsters, most of whom continued to be naughty. Those who have portraits of their nineteenth-century European ancestors hanging on the wall can understand why those folks never smiled. But if scaring the devil out of sinners worked, the church would have stomped out sin long ago.

The *Struwwelpeter* rationale continues today in programs like Scared Straight, where older adult inmates scare youths through threats of rape and beatings that occur in prison. The theory is that these potential horrors will frighten young rebels out of getting into more trouble. But that approach has never been an effective early intervention strategy for the same reason that mandatory sentencing and capital punishment have not deterred people from committing crimes. Most people just do not think that far ahead, and even those who do, do not think that they will be caught. Even worse, many youths are simply attracted to the challenge of being tougher or "beating the system."

Requirements for Effective Punishment

The most frequent question we receive when discussing alternatives to punishment is "Don't children need consequences?" Technically, all behavior has *some* consequence, so the question really means "Don't children need *punishments?*" Certainly, children need to learn that their behavior can have specific damaging consequences. No society could exist without sanctions for behavior that violates others. Some punishment should be inescapable because of the serious nature of certain acts.

Even when punishment is inevitable, we should not assume that simply administering punishment will necessarily teach the right lesson. Punishments may be effective, or at least not harmful, when given in the context of a caring relationship. However, punishment often backfires with many unintended side effects when administered to troubled youths. The following list contains the components of effective punishment, but also some of the unintended consequences which often happen with troubled youth.

PRINCIPLES OF EFFECTIVE PUNISHMENT	UNINTENDED CONSEQUENCES
1. Youth experiences displeasure from acts such as physical punishment, loss of privileges, or timeout.	Troubled youths may seem impervious to the pain of punishment or may even enjoy battles with adults, isolation, or masochistic suffering.
2. The displeasure causes frustration and the normal emotional response of anger.	Some who have been cruelly treated by adults feel they are being attacked. They respond with violent fury or try to escape by withdrawing or running away.
3. Youth can distinguish between the source of displeasure (the punisher) and the cause (one's own behavior).	Many delinquent youth have learned to deny responsibility for their own problems and instead project blame on the punishing adult for their difficulty.
4. Youth responds by getting mad at him- or herself rather than the punisher.	Many troubled youth nurture a desire for vengeance against the punisher or see punishment as proof that they are bad and worthless. When they turn their anger inward, they become self-destructive.
5. The youth feels remorse and vows to reform: "I won't do something dumb like this again."	Youth who do not recognize a problem or accept responsibility for it may not experience remorse. Instead, they may become sneakier, vowing, "I won't be so dumb as to get caught next time."
6. When next facing temptation, the youth recalls the previous incident and exercises self-control.	A youth whose conscience is weak does not learn from the punishment experience, but may feel guilt only after the fact. A youth with a numb conscience may feel guilt only after the fact and then act out more to provoke punishment.[1]

From Northern Ireland, delinquency expert Michael Montgomery tells of a practice that was once widely used by the Irish Republican Army to punish youthful car thieves, called "joy riders." These delinquents were taken out into the country where they were "knee-capped"—crippled by shooting them in the knees. But as soon as they left the hospital in casts and on crutches, the first thing they would do is steal another car and race through Belfast with angry pride. Says Michael Montgomery, "With our most difficult youth, punishment is powerless."[2]

Most youth coming out of jail say that they will never commit another crime because they do not want to be locked up again. But if simply "not getting caught" is their only motivation, it seldom works. Troubled youth must have something much bigger to say "yes" to than just the fear of getting caught. Simply trying to eliminate everything bad from someone's life, without replacing it with something good, merely leaves a person feeling *empty*. And nobody will stay empty for very long. Unfortunately, many of our "crime-fighting" strategies promise emptiness at best. We must also think about what we ultimately hope to accomplish with punishment. Is it merely to satisfy our need for revenge, or is it to work for positive change in the offender as well?

Labeled for Life

Danny was released from a juvenile facility and placed into one of Straight Ahead's aftercare homes. Within a few weeks, a girl in the community took a keen interest in him, though her motives were self-serving. She wanted to use Danny to make her boyfriend jealous. She said she needed to talk with Danny and asked that he meet her at a friend's house. They ended up having sex, and Danny left shortly thereafter.

What happened later that night became a nightmare. The girl called her boyfriend to tell him what had happened. Rather than trying to get her back, he said he never wanted to see her again. She began drinking excessive amounts of alcohol until she had to be taken to the hospital. Upon examination, they discovered that she had engaged in sexual intercourse. Feeling too embarrassed to tell her mother the truth, she said she had been raped.

Danny was arrested the next day. Upon further investigation, each witness confirmed that the girl had seduced Danny, asking him to have sex with her. It was clear that, at the very least, the act was consensual. All charges were to be dropped, or so we thought.

The detective pointed out that because Danny was 16 years old and the girl only 15, she could not legally give consent to sexual intercourse. Therefore, he would still be charged with statutory rape. To make matters more complicated, under new state laws, *any* type of sexual offense required automatic adult sentencing.

Consequently, Danny was locked up again, losing his job and school standing. The case went on for more than a year, when eventually Danny was found guilty of statutory rape, but kept in the juvenile courts. They reasoned that once he turned 18, the case would be sealed as part of his juvenile record.

No one would dispute the fact that Danny did something wrong. And he learned a painful lesson. But who could have foreseen how the wrongful act of a 16-year-old would continue to haunt him well into his 40s?

A new law was passed in Danny's home state, which mandated that everyone with any sexual offense must publicly register as a "sex offender," for 20 years. Danny has become a model citizen, has graduated *summa cum laude* from a liberal arts college, and is now nearing graduation from graduate school.

Whatever profession Danny enters, he will likely be subject to background checks. Because his state's sex offender registry does not distinguish between different levels of sexual offenses, he may well be denied employment. And so, Danny, like thousands of other juveniles with similar charges, is a modern-day leper—an outcast of society. Though these individuals may feel remorse and straighten out their lives, their penance is never complete.

Punishment Versus Rehabilitation

Today we know more than ever before about the science of what works in the prevention and treatment of delinquency, yet we are turning our backs on our most troubled and troubling youth. Large numbers of juveniles are now being tried in adult courts and serving time in adult prisons. This punishment erases any distinction between the needs of adult criminals and young offenders and deprives them of protections usually afforded children. Because most citizens care deeply about all children, such destructive practices can only be maintained if there is widespread public ignorance and misinformation. Several common myths justify efforts to regress to an era when youth were handled like adult criminals.

Myth 1: Juvenile courts were not designed for today's serious delinquents.

Some argue that today's juveniles need adult courts because they are a violent breed, while those of yesteryear merely engaged in boyish pranks like stealing hubcaps. A widely quoted "study" suggests that in past generations, the most serious school problems were gum chewing and throwing spit wads, but that modern teachers more commonly face problems like assault and rape.

In fact, a careful search by social scientist Michael Males determined that even though the findings of this study were widely quoted, no such study ever existed. Perhaps such misinformation is not challenged because elders in every generation are inclined to minimize their own youthful indiscretions while magnifying the faults of the younger generation.

Nevertheless, every generation has had its core of violent young persons, although they have always been a small minority. Violent youths were around when the juvenile court was formed in 1899 as well. Jane Addams described Chicago in that era as a dangerous place where kids killing kids with guns was an almost daily occurrence.

She documented gang violence, revolt in classrooms, addiction, and widespread crime, even among girls. The big difference between delinquents then and now was color. Troubled youths in earlier generations were mainly children of recent European immigrants. Miss Addams mobilized prominent Chicago women to create the juvenile court so that these new young citizens could also realize the American dream.

Justice with compassion was the mission of the modern juvenile court. Almost all juvenile courts are descended from the first one founded in Chicago in 1899. Yet few who criticize juvenile courts have ever read the following document:

The Juvenile Court Purpose: Cook County, Illinois, 1899

1. To secure for each minor subject hereto such care and guidance, preferably in his own home, as will serve the moral, emotional, mental, and physical welfare of the minor and the best interests of the community.

2. To preserve and strengthen the minor's family ties whenever possible, removing him from the custody of his parents only when his welfare or safety or the protection of the public cannot be adequately safeguarded without removal.

3. When the minor is removed from his own family, to secure for him custody, care, and discipline as nearly as possible equivalent to that which should be given by his parents.

The original juvenile court philosophy is relevant today because it embodies key democratic principles of minimal governmental interference, the primacy of the family, placement in the least-restrictive alternative setting, and the responsibility of the community for all of its children. This document ranks with the Magna Carta and other great human rights statements. Its principles have been adopted by democracies worldwide and are part of the protections guaranteed children under international law. When this philosophy is abandoned, we step back from treating all children as our children. Which of the principles in these questions would we be willing to compromise for our own son or daughter?

Does only my child need positive guidance for moral, physical, and mental growth?

Would I allow the state to take away my responsibility for parenting my child if removal was not absolutely necessary?

If my child had to be placed, should government be permitted to provide a quality of care or discipline less than that expected from a good parent?

Myth 2: Youth crime rates are higher than ever before.

Rates of delinquency go in cycles, tracking family and community anomie, such as are caused by unemployment and conflicts of cultural values. The end of the nineteenth century was marked by urban poverty and ethnic unrest among immigrants, and rates of delinquency, drug abuse, and suicide soared. The newly created juvenile courts, child guidance clinics, and a national program of recreation and youth development supported families and, in time, contributed to lower delinquency rates.

Delinquency spiked again in the 1930s because of a worldwide depression, which again caused unemployment and social upheaval. Crime peaked in 1935 when millions of troublemaking youths roamed cities or rode the rails. Many labeled them "the lost generation." However, citizens again responded with massive investments in youth development infrastructure. Larry Brendtro's father was reclaimed in the "million boy army" of the Civilian Conservation Corps. This big investment paid off, for this lost generation would save the world for democracy in World War II. Tom Brokaw honors them as *The Greatest Generation* in his inspiring 1998 book by that title.

High levels of delinquency returned in the 1970s and 1980s. Closing factories made unskilled urban males casualties of the information society and further disrupted family stability. A new generation of fatherless African American children was recruited and armed by adult entrepreneurs in the illicit drug industry. Crack cocaine did something neither slavery nor poverty could do. It caused many African American mothers and others to abandon their children. As a result, urban youth crime rocketed, while in stable families and communities, the problems were less pronounced.

How did the nation respond? For the first time in American history, delinquency was seen as a problem of the "disadvantaged," a euphemism for African American children. White fear of Black crime was exploited for political advantage. Liberals and conservatives competed to out-tough one another with slogans like "do adult crime, and you'll do adult time." Also new to the equation were profit-making corrections companies. Even as crime rates dropped, this insatiable "government-industrial corrections complex" devoured billions of tax dollars needed for schools and youth development.

Myth 3: "Nothing works" to rehabilitate delinquents.

In the 1970s, an article by sociologist Robert Martinson planted the pernicious idea that delinquents could not be rehabilitated.[3] This fiction spread like wildfire even though later studies debunked this notion, and Martinson himself claimed he was misinterpreted. A mass of research and practical wisdom shows that even delinquents who are serious offenders can often be turned around. Based on what we know about prevention science, we need a three-pronged initiative on juvenile crime: prevention, early intervention, and the restoration of social bonds.

Prevention. The highest priority should be interventions to ensure that all children are reared in consistent, safe, and loving environments. They need to feel they belong in many places: home, school, positive peer groups, and neighborhoods. Schools must help children develop self-discipline so that they can act responsibly even in conflicts. Churches need to offer all children—especially those from troubled backgrounds—an island of peace in a sea of conflict and a reflection of hope in the faces of adults who care for them.

Early intervention. Children at risk can often be identified as early as kindergarten, and their families can be given parent education and support. Neglected and abused children must be drawn into supportive relationships with stable members of communities and churches. Millions of children are stigmatized because their parents are in prison or are facing other perils. Bully prevention research shows that half of all middle school bullies will have adult felony records by age 24 if they do not receive intervention. Communities must make special efforts to mentor children of poverty and color, because these students desperately need the opportunities afforded by education.

Restoration of social bonds. With our most damaged youth, the only real choice is between reclaiming or discarding them. Those who cause the greatest concern are those angry youths who roam our streets or are incarcerated in juvenile jails. There are many promising programs for this population, but all require caring adults and an attention to values as well as behavior. Even with our most difficult youth, research shows that many can be reclaimed. At the end of a decade of studying incarcerated delinquent youths, Martin Gold, of the University of Michigan, concludes that we must reduce their psychological and social isolation and invite them to return to us as responsible members of the community.[4]

Myth 4: The Bible calls for "an eye for an eye."

Many have used Biblical laws like an "eye for an eye, tooth for a tooth"[5] as a basis for a "get tough on crime" stance, reasoning that this is how God works. Unfortunately, they do not realize that this command was actually given as a call to mercy. It was a call to make the punishment fit the crime, for people of that day were stoning to death those who stole. Some felt justified in killing an entire family or tribe as retaliation for the offence of one individual. So the purpose of this law was not to increase the penalty, but to limit the punishment to the level of the offense.

While the Bible is strong on justice and punishment, it is also balanced with mercy and restoration. Many passages display God's heart toward the oppressed and imprisoned. For example, "The Lord looked down from his sanctuary on high, from heaven he viewed the earth, to hear the groans of the prisoners and release those condemned to death."6

In fact, throughout the Bible, God seems to actively seek out at least five distinct groups of people: the poor, the sick, the orphaned, the widowed, and the imprisoned. Most troubled youths fit several of these categories. God has always chosen the "low, despised, foolish things of the world to confound the wise."7

Interestingly, there seems to be something about age 20 in Scripture which indicates a greater level of accountability as well as some degree of innocence for those younger than 20. In referring to the children of Israel's lack of faith for moving into the Promised Land, God said, "Because they have not followed me wholeheartedly, not one of the men twenty years old or more who came up out of Egypt will see the land I promised on oath to Abraham, Isaac and Jacob."8 Likewise, King David pleads with God, asking him to "remember not the sins of my youth and my rebellious ways; according to your love remember me, for you are good, O Lord."9

We now know that the last part of the brain to develop in humans is the ability to handle ambiguous information and make logical, coherent decisions. Neuroscientists have confirmed that the part of the brain where judgments are formed, the prefrontal cortex, is not fully developed in most people until their early 20s. During adolescence, the limbic system, where raw emotions such as anger are generated, enters a stage of hyperdevelopment, explaining at least in part how teens can be so moody, apparently making decisions based solely on emotions.10

Myth 5: Imprisonment is an economically viable crime prevention strategy.

The political rhetoric of "do adult crime, do adult time" is popular, but it contradicts both the science of youth development and conservative economic beliefs. In no other area of government would citizens tolerate such a waste of public money without positive outcomes. Most citizens are unaware that "lock 'em up" laws have fostered a highly profitable prison-industrial complex and an out-of-control raid on taxpayers. The facts are shown in the following statistics.

PRISON ECONOMICS 101

- In the U.S., taxpayers spend twice as much on crime as crime costs.

- Get-tough laws increased prison capacity 700% in just one generation.

- More than half of all prisoners are serving time for offenses costing less than $1,000.

- The U.S. jails four times as many persons proportionately as the country with the second-highest jail rate, New Zealand.

- A majority of persons entering prison are employed, but 66% will be unemployed 6 months after release.

- Youth are 5 times more likely to be raped and 7.7 times more likely to kill themselves if placed in adult prisons rather than in juvenile facilities.

- When released, youth who were incarcerated in adult prisons are statistically more likely to reoffend than if they had been placed in juvenile facilities.

Even greater than the economic loss is the human waste. The main way youth are protected from victimization in adult prisons is to segregate them in solitary confinement or "the hole." Medical research shows that solitary confinement causes health and psychiatric deterioration in many prisoners within as little as 24 hours.

In its report on human rights violations of youth in the U.S. justice system, Amnesty International describes the widespread use of such practices, which violate international conventions against torture. Approaching this issue from a conservative perspective, criminologist John DiIulio concludes:

> Most kids who get into serious trouble with the law need adult guidance, and they won't find suitable role models in prison. Jailing youth with adult felons under Spartan conditions will merely produce more street gladiators.[11]

Placing young offenders in adult prisons increases, not lessens, their propensity for committing crime, for while in prison, the juvenile offender learns from older, more hardened criminals. And when they are released back into the community in their 20s—undereducated, unsocialized, unemployable, and at the peak of their physical power—we will have created the very person we wanted most to avoid. One shudders to imagine the long-term effect of such short-sightedness—not only for a generation of youth condemned to prison, but for all who will be left with a more violent society.

GROWING UP IN PRISON
By Tony Rios

I was barely 15 years old when I walked into the prison. At first I was still in a state of shock, desperately trying not to believe that this was truly happening to me. But it was very much real and true. I was strip-searched—for security reasons I was told. About this point I was dazed and confused and felt so alone. I feared what the prison had in store for me.

After two weeks in the tank, I was sent to the minimum-security prison because of my age. I stayed there for nine months with nothing but time on my hands. I was too young to qualify for any of the classes or trades they had to offer, so I started to get a lot of minor write-ups because I had nothing to do. This resulted in my being sent to the main prison, where I had never been. After about two months, I got into a fight with three inmates. I got badly beaten because I refused to be strong-armed or bullied. My cousin was stabbed to death in the same prison.

At this point in time, I began to miss my family and my mom, but they were too far away to come console me. Before I was taken to the hole because of a fight, I attempted to take my life. I felt as if no one cared any more so why not? A riot started and I became involved.

I knew I could be charged and face life in prison, but it was better than having anyone pick on me. Even though I was in a gang now, the gang members weren't always around to protect me. After the riot, I was placed in the hole where I stayed for 14 straight months. Then I was placed in administrative segregation for 10 more months. At this point I had spent my 16th, 17th, and 18th birthdays in the hole or administrative segregation.

I didn't care what I did, or if anything happened to me or to those I was related to. I had learned to shut all emotions off, because that way I wouldn't feel the pain of loneliness for my family. I felt alone, confused, and depressed and the feeling of emptiness still haunts me to this day, four years later.

Building more prisons and juvenile facilities won't work as a deterrent to crime. The money being spent for all this building should be used for better education and counseling for those youth who are falling into the wrong tracks in life. Prisons are a training ground for the young people who enter their gates. Once these kids graduate, they will commit more heinous crimes because they have received advanced psychological training in the criminal way of thinking.

At first this place changed me into this unremorseful monster who would fight at the drop of a hat and didn't care about myself or anyone in general. It hardened me on the inside to a point that no one could get through to me with anything about where I was going in life. There was no one I could talk to who would listen with an open heart instead of an open book listing rules and prisoners. All I ever wanted was for someone to listen, someone who would understand what was going through my mind.[12]

Searching for a Better Way

The point of all this is not to ignore the consequences for evil or to ignore justice. For as C. S. Lewis said, "Mercy detached from justice grows unmerciful." Rather, we must ask, "What is the most *just* thing we can do for the sake of everyone involved?"

In times of crisis, there is a loss of the spirit of hope within many of our communities. In its place is the sense that there are no workable solutions to the massive social problems facing society. Feeling helpless, one can easily become paralyzed and retreat into inaction. Or one can strike out at those who aggress against society—giving up on and abandoning those who have given up on themselves.

The Failure of Retribution and Rehabilitation

Debates on delinquency have always been driven more by emotion than logic. One side attacks the weakness of *bleeding hearts* who show sympathy to delinquents. The other side attributes *hardness of heart* to persons who will not understand or forgive. Locked into opposing mindsets, the approach to troubled youth has whipsawed for a century between retribution and rehabilitation. Perhaps it is time to declare a draw, admitting that both sides have lost the debate.

Throughout the twentieth century, the juvenile courts, with mixed results, offered young lawbreakers a combination of punishment, treatment, and counseling to straighten out their lives. As the new millennium begins, large numbers of U.S. juveniles arrested for violent and nonviolent crimes are being placed in adult prisons, and death penalties are given to scores of our most violent youth.

Although such sentences of a child are in violation of international law, as recognized by the consciences of most of the world's democracies, they have become commonplace in parts of the United States. The most severe sentences are disproportionately doled out to children of poverty and color.

Does retribution really work? Jesse Williams, a Philadelphia youth corrections official, does not think so: "Tough speeches may be good for politicians' re-elections, but they don't make much sense for curbing the cycle of juvenile crime." Crime consultant Donna Hamparian of Columbus, Ohio, agrees: "As more and more youths are put behind bars, the projected violator totals are so high that we can't build enough prisons to keep all of them locked up."[13] The reality is that even if more youth are put into adult prisons, the vast majority will still be released to society and then be more violent and dangerous than ever.

But does rehabilitation as it has been practiced really work? In many respects, advocates of rehabilitation have been as pessimistic in their own way as have proponents of punishment. Once promising rehabilitation programs have deteriorated into negative and oppressive rituals, even when presided over by kindly persons who call themselves "helping" professionals.

Most traditional treatment approaches are variations of "flaw-fixing." Professionals who view delinquents as patients, victims, disturbed, or disordered share a pessimism on a par with those who advocate retribution. Because most treatment is a variant of control psychology, delinquents do not rush with open arms to their therapists any more than they would rush to their wardens.

Why "Tit for Tat" Has Failed

Most people adhere to the moral principle of "do to others as they do to you," which is not as close to the Golden Rule as it first sounds. Are we obligated only to befriend those who act friendly and to express hostility to those who are hostile? This is the ancient folk logic underlying the phrase "just deserts."

Canadian game theorist Anatol Rapaport built a computer simulation to demonstrate that "do to others as they do to you" is the dominant model for human social relations. He labels this simple program in full capitals as the TIT FOR TAT rule. It says that we as human beings reciprocate kindness as well as hostility. One good turn—or bad turn—deserves another.[14]

Tit for tat certainly fosters social harmony much better than simply distrusting everybody, and it gives rise to small bands of cooperative persons who learn to trust one another and live in peace. But because it also prescribes "getbacks" among enemies, reciprocal retribution can continue unabated, just as it did in the feud between the Hatfields and McCoys.

As Australian criminologist David Moore observes, the notion that the cure must take a similar form to the disease is typical of magical thinking. By this logic of reciprocal retribution, each party is entitled to hurt the other. Gordon McLean, who heads the Juvenile Justice Ministry with Youth for Christ in Chicago, says that many victims of violence "want to strike out in understandable rage at the offender, seeking closure in places it can't be found—a courtroom or an execution chamber."[15] But as Sister Helen Prejean describes in *Dead Man Walking*, even when a victim's relatives watch the execution of the murderer, this does nothing to heal them of that crime.

Tit for tat was designed to operate in a simple human ecology. It actually worked quite well throughout most of human history under these conditions:

- People lived in small tribes or kinship bands. The word "enemy" and "stranger" were synonymous, so driving them away or killing them secured the community.

- Subjects willingly submitted to authority. Children politely obeyed—as did slaves, serfs, and wives—and the despot was kind and benevolent. Tit for tat ruled.

Though we may still tend toward tit for tat, it is poorly matched to today's complex world. Is there a better way?

Progressive Models of Reconciliation

The failure of traditional retribution and rehabilitation is the failure of tit for tat. Behaviorist B. F. Skinner showed that punishment triggers unintended side effects such as fighting back or running away. And before you know it, positive reinforcement, the mainstay of behavior modification, gives way to locked isolation and a menu of punishments politely called "behavior decreasers."

Therapists become experts at behavior management, but delinquents are even more expert at manipulation. Zero tolerance principals patrol the hallways while students scribble graffiti in the bathroom stalls. The warden cracks down, and the inmate underground fights back. Peer counseling groups mutate into angry high-decibel verbal warfare. Tit for tat fails if there is a program for warfare but no mechanism for reconciliation.

The Antidote to Tit for Tat

There is a better way. The limits of tit for tat have been obvious to wise persons for millennia. Tribal traditions used reconciliation as a means of conflict resolution. Scripture presented a theology of forgiveness, which could ultimately bring about the potential for reconciliation. And more recently, reconciliation has become a more dominant theme for new models of justice, counseling, group work, and reeducation. These models all share a common theme. In the terminology of people of faith, the antidote to the power of tit for tat can be written boldly: **repentance, forgiveness,** and **reconciliation.**

In reconciliation, the offender experiences remorse, repents, and seeks to make amends. Those hurt by the offender directly experience this transformation and may even be able to move from hatred to forgiveness. This powerful spiritual transformation is prominent throughout the Bible. Joseph was sold into slavery by jealous older brothers, but 20 years later he had the opportunity to pay them back. Starving like the prodigal son, they begged to be his slaves. But after calculating a process to determine and assure his brothers' true repentance, Joseph simply forgave them and welcomed them as brothers.[16] In the Beatitudes, Jesus revokes the tit for tat rule with his mandate that his followers love their enemies as well as their neighbors.[17]

Reconciliation is the only hope for healing the deep wounds of violence, fear, and prejudice. John Dawson defines genuine reconciliation as expressing and receiving forgiveness, and as pursuing friendship with previous enemies.[18]

A Historical Perspective

Throughout the long history of humanity, most people survived as hunter-gatherers and lived in communities of only a few hundred people. In such societies, it was not feasible to lock up criminals, and killing or banishing them was also quite rare. As Charles Colson and Daniel Van Ness explain, prisons were largely a contrivance of despotic kings and lords of castles who tried to keep control of their stolen empires. Instead of resolving the problem between the offender and victim, the state exercised its power and imposed arbitrary punishments.[19]

Outside of Europe, clans and kinship communities thrived until modern times. In many different cultures, tribal peoples developed ceremonies for bringing victim and offender together to restore harmony. In the communities of believers in the Bible, there were rituals for confronting sinners who were disrupting the community. The goal was to convey how the offender had hurt others and to secure genuine repentance and a commitment to reform.

Today there are a number of exciting alternatives to tit for tat justice. We briefly examine three of these models, which are finding widespread application with troubled kids. These include the restorative justice model, counseling strategies that use crisis as an opportunity, and group treatment models that enlist youth in peer helping groups.

1. Restorative Justice

Justice officials the world over are rediscovering the power of traditional systems of victim-offender reconciliation. This is an alternative to retributive strategies that fail to heal victims or reform offenders. A pioneer in this effort was Australian criminologist John Braithwaite, who adapted methods used by the Maori in New Zealand for use in a modern society. These principles have been called restorative justice and are based on "reintegrative shaming."

Reconciliation is the goal of rehabilitation programs that bring victim and offender together. The offender is confronted with how he or she has hurt another person. Feeling genuine shame and empathy for the victim, the offender confesses the wrongdoing and apologizes to the victim, then seeks to make amends through restitution or compensation to victims and through a commitment to a transformed life. The victim is healed, and the offender is forgiven and restored to the community. The Bible is filled with examples of sinners who have been reclaimed through this process.

Unfortunately, most shaming done today is not integrative. Rituals used to stigmatize and cut the violator off forever, as in the Jewish qetsateh ceremony at the time of the prodigal son. Such a process is a perversion of reintegrative shaming and cannot be expected to achieve positive ends. While the Bible clearly reserves vengeance to God, people have long wanted to play God. Similarly, any current programs for criminal offenders seem designed mainly to humiliate them. This serves to drive them from the community bond and to revoke their status as a neighbor.

Shame, which causes a person to feel both psychological and physical distress, is among the most powerful of our biologically based emotions. As Australian criminologist David Moore notes, learning what is and is not shameful is an important part of moral development. These experiences are what often cause a person to avoid crime. For most people, believing criminal acts are repugnant prevents them from committing crimes, even if they could avoid detection. And if they err, shame causes them to seek forgiveness and reconciliation.

But shame can go awry. In some people, it is triggered too easily, as when an abused child feels shame because of the actions of an abuser. Distorted shame can cause a person to feel flawed and to feel that *he or she* is a mistake rather than seeing that their *wrongdoing* is the mistake. In contrast, some delinquents take no responsibility for hurting others, and we say they are "shameless."

Current systems of justice make crime a face-off between the state and the delinquent. When government assumes this role, it deprives offenders of the opportunity to directly experience how their behaviors have hurt members of the community. Victims also become sidelined and do not have a chance to understand what really happened or to express their anger and hurt. Likewise, the offender usually goes through a trial without taking the stand and may end up feeling resentment instead of shame. Even harsh sentences may only fuel a desire to strike back in angry pride.

Shaming that seeks to reclaim is one of the most powerful crime-fighting tools ever created. Shaming that only stigmatizes and banishes is equally powerful, but in a negative sense: it is designed to destroy a person's sense of relatedness and self-worth. The intent of restorative justice is to address the needs of the victim as well as those of the offender. While demanding the offender assume responsibility for his or her actions, the intent is not to permanently stigmatize and banish this brother or sister from the family. Only when penitence is linked with reconciliation can victims, offenders, and communities heal.

Meeting my victim. Rob had racked up a long list of delinquent charges by the time he was 16, and had been in and out of a myriad of groups and programs, but to no avail. Some had labeled him as a youth without a conscience. Finally, one of his crimes changed him forever. Here is Rob's story:

> My friends and I were walking down the street when we saw the window down on a Volvo. I reached in and grabbed a cellular phone that was sitting on the seat. We had done stuff like that so many times we didn't even look to see if anyone was watching. That's why we were so surprised when the owner of the car started yelling at us from across the street.

We took off running and threw the phone on the ground. Then he started chasing us. I knew he had gotten a good look at us all, and I figured he would probably go turn us in to the police.

The next day someone knocked at our door. I looked out the window and recognized the person as the man whose car we broke into. Now I was really scared. I had friends who had been shot for less than this. My mother told me to answer the door. "No!" I said. "I know that guy, and I don't want to see him!"

I couldn't believe she opened the door and let him right into the house. He said he lived a few blocks away and had seen me around the neighborhood. Then he explained to her what I had done and that he wanted to talk to me. I was petrified when she made me come out and talk to him.

"Son," he said, "I don't want to get off on the wrong foot with you, but I want you to know why I have a cellular phone. My wife is due to have a baby any day, and I want her to be able to reach me if she needs to get into the hospital."

Then he told me that he owned a pizza place down the street and invited me to come in some time for a free Coke. I said, "Sure. Thanks a lot. And I'm sorry about your phone." Then he left.

I never took him up on his offer, 'cause I would be too embarrassed. But that's the last time I ever stole anything from anyone. I still can't believe how that guy treated me. But it made me not want to hurt anybody else.

Rob's powerful encounter with his victim is a straightforward example of how *understanding the consequences* of behavior can sometimes serve as an even stronger deterrent than *administering consequences.*

2. Crisis as Opportunity

Problems are a normal part of living and can be used as tremendous occasions for learning and growth. We were created to be problem solvers, which is part of what we do all day long at school or in our work. Then we come home and do crossword puzzles, learn how to skateboard, or struggle with a new computer program. And when we have not solved a problem, it keeps popping up in our mind until we sometimes discover answers to unsolved problems in our dreams!

Some psychologists contend that solving problems is the most basic activity of the human brain. Therefore, developing competence in our youth involves teaching them to cultivate their resilience and creatively cope with life's challenges. Mutual problem solving based on respectful communication is a far more potent basis for change than is coercion. As Archbishop Desmond Tutu has said, "Intimidation is merely an acknowledgment of the weakness of your point of view."[20]

As we have discussed, tit for tat only causes both children and adults to become hooked into nonproductive conflict cycles. Research has shown that serious school conflicts, including those that result in violent crimes, often begin small but escalate to tragic results. Based on careful study of thousands of conflicts with troubled children, Nicholas Long and Mary Wood have developed specific strategies for disengaging from these conflict cycles and communicating with kids in crisis.

The Conflict Cycle. The conflict cycle is a useful model for understanding how conflicts develop and get out of control. As illustrated in the following figure, (1) *stress* leads to (2) *feelings* such as anger or depression, which trigger (3) *behavior* that in turn elicits (4) *reactions* from adults or peers. These reactions can trigger more stress and the conflict cycles can continue until what started as a small incident escalates into a major crisis. Adults need to understand the conflict cycle to avoid futile power struggles. Young people also need to learn how to disengage from conflict lest their anger propel them into aggressive and even violent acts.

THE CONFLICT CYCLE

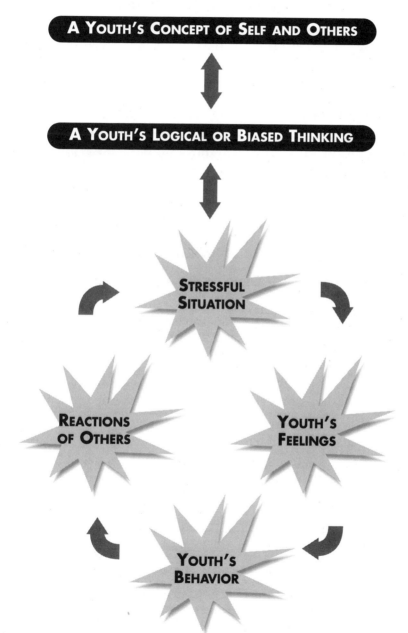

The Conflict Cycle is used with permission from the Life Space Crisis Intervention Institute.

Conflicts and discipline problems can be used as unique opportunities for learning and growth. Instead of becoming locked in combat, the adult assumes the role of a coach, guiding the youth, who can then examine how he or she continues to fall into patterns of self-defeating behavior.

Even if behavior requires a consequence, we can still use this method as a chance to explore how the youth continues to get into these difficulties. Simplistic reward-punishment schemes often fail with difficult children because they ignore the distorted thinking or values that drive problem behavior. Adults need skills in dealing with such problems as self-centered thinking, a lack of guilt, being easily misled by peers, and getting into conflict cycles. When adults connect with kids in conflict, relationships are strengthened, but this requires skills at defusing anger and enlisting youth in shared problem solving.

A roadmap for talking to youth in crisis. One of the most useful processes for solving problems we have encountered is a system called Life Space Crisis Intervention (LSCI), which is built around the conflict cycle.[21] Developed by Mary Wood and Nicholas Long, LSCI makes use of a natural problem in the "life space" of participants by turning it into a teaching opportunity. It is not therapy, although it is very therapeutic. While advanced training and certification is available for teachers, principals, counselors, pastors, and others who want advanced skills, the foundation skills of LSCI are teachable to any intelligent person.

In LSCI, the adult becomes a coach and the youth in conflict becomes the expert. Most youth like coaches because they know the coach is trying to help them develop their strengths, helping them become the best they can be. Many youth are wary of counselors or therapists because they see them as trying to uncover their weaknesses.

Young people who resist formal counseling are much more likely to participate in this process. Notice how it works, in this simple, abbreviated, four-step format:

1. Defusing the conflict

2. Building a time line of the conflict

3. Understanding what causes the conflict

4. Resolving the conflict

An example of LSCI being used in a crisis situation is provided in Appendix C.

3. Peer Helping Groups

Whatever the stated philosophy, every program for troubled youth produces a potent peer-group culture, often negative. Many adults tolerate this counterculture and others fight against it. A better option is to capitalize on the peer-group dynamics and enlist youth as active change agents and partners in their own healing. While there are many peer counseling models, we would distinguish between those based on peer coercion and those based on peer concern. Only the latter would qualify as programs of reconciliation.

Peer helping groups, sometimes called Positive Peer Culture or PPC, have been used in a variety of mental health, correctional, educational, and treatment settings. Positive Peer Culture attempts to teach the basic value of caring for one another. The primary technique for teaching this value is the use of peer helping groups wherein both staff and peers identify problems displayed by group members and develop strategies to solve those problems. Troubled youth are considered to have the potential for strength and greatness instead of the more typical view of them as being negative and destructive.

Three strategies dominate these peer-group programs: modeling caring, demanding responsibility, and solving problems.

Modeling caring. An authoritative, but not authoritarian, adult models caring behavior and expects the same from youth. Refusing to become ensnared in a power struggle with a negative group, adults instead challenge the group. Even the most difficult and rebellious students are seen as having potential for helping.

Adults are not pushovers, and they have high expectations that youth will help and not hurt one another. When problems do occur, they are handled in the group so that the offender is confronted with the impact his or her behavior had on others.

Adults keep the process from becoming negative by modeling respectful caring behavior and expecting the same from youth, by demanding responsibility instead of obedience from youth. Since youth want to be respected and treated with maturity, in time, most are drawn into positive roles. In effect, they become partners with staff and peers working for their own healing.

Demanding responsibility. Troubled youth do not respond well to either permissive, punitive, or arrogant adults. Youth quickly are drawn into conflict with any adult they see as punitive or arrogant. But they also take advantage of a weak adult, who becomes a scapegoat for residual anger earned by other adults in their lives. Thus, the ideal adult role demands responsibility rather than obedience.

Because youth want to be independent, this demand is palatable. The adult also needs to ensure that youth do not avoid ownership of their problems. Through methods of reversing responsibility, adults and group members make each youth own up to his or her hurtful behavior. A young person who says "My parents don't care about me; why should I care?" will be confronted by a chorus of youth giving a message such as "We're not talking about your parents' problems, but yours, and only you can take charge of your life."

Solving problems. In regular group meetings, each member has the obligation and opportunity to share problems seen in self and others. As group trust develops, young people become very involved in helping one another, even when this includes respectful confrontation about how a person is hurting another. In this process, something very similar to tribal reconciliation results. The offender becomes aware of how his or her behavior has affected others in the group, so that strong feelings of remorse, empathy, and attachment may develop.

Peer culture groups are often used in combination with the programs for reeducation described in the next chapter. Research by John Gibbs at Ohio State University found that peer helping could be enhanced by the addition of programs like EQUIP, which give youth more skills as helpers through additional training in moral decision making, anger management, and social skills.

The Courage to Forgive

In his book, *Living Faith*, former President Jimmy Carter laments the fact that our society seems to have strayed from the concepts of forgiveness and reconciliation. Concerned about the cynicism of government, Carter illustrates how it has become more popular for a governor to boast of building prison cells than schoolrooms:

> When governments reach their limits, the teachings of Jesus Christ and the prophets of other faiths must prevail: "You shall love the Lord your God—and your neighbor as yourself." We have a much greater opportunity beyond government to have our hearts united, to reach out personally to those in need, and to expand our lives in demonstrating self-sacrificing love, love for the unlovable.[22]

Strategies that turn conflict into reconciliation are needed. Three such models have been highlighted, including restorative justice, crisis as opportunity, and peer helping groups. All of these approaches involve mutual problem solving and direct, but respectful, communication on how a person's behavior has hurt another person. Such encounters are far more effective than coercion.

Baptist minister Bernice King lost both her famous father as well as her grandmother to violent murders. In her ministry with youth in Atlanta, she tells them of the importance of learning to overcome the tendency to hate those whose behavior hurts us. Intervening without violence is an art of great courage, not weakness. Only by confronting evil acts, instead of those who commit them, will we be able to heal our victims, offenders, and communities.

CHAPTER 10

Redeeming

cultivating commitment

My soul was famished within me, for want of that spiritual food.

—Saint Augustine, theologian and philosopher
(354–430)

MODERN YOUTH ARE SUFFERING from a deep spiritual hunger. Yet most schools are so narrowly preoccupied with academic achievement and superficial behavior that they fail to meet the most basic emotional and spiritual needs of their children. Likewise, many courts are no longer committed to meeting the needs of our most difficult children. Even professional counselors may not know how to speak to the hearts of the youth they serve.

Appearing before the American Psychiatric Association, M. Scott Peck indicted his colleagues for actively disregarding spirituality. Peck suggested that many were avoiding spiritual issues because they are products of a narrow "value-free" scientism that declares spiritual matters out of bounds. He offered guidelines for inquiring about this area of a person's life, just as a counselor might gather a social or educational history.[1]

Now, as the frantic pace and complexity of modern life upsets our balance, we strive to correct our course and rediscover a purpose for living. Such has always been the case with our most troubled youth who find little hope in their lives and are compelled at a young age to ask deeply spiritual questions. Today, even secular researchers recognize the importance of integrating the spiritual dimension into a holistic approach to positive youth development. Concepts such as virtue, faith, and forgiveness are taking center stage as we realize the emptiness of a *do your own thing* world.

Ministering to Spiritual Needs

In our experience, the majority of high-risk youth are far more spiritually hungry than the general youth population. A person will ask many more questions when in trouble than when life is going well. Yet care professionals generally try to avoid discussions about faith with young people.

Because of their unfulfilled hunger, many troubled young people begin to dabble in the occult in an attempt to satisfy their yearnings. As a result, they are often more familiar with the spiritual realm than those who are counseling them.

Psychiatrist Robert Coles has studied the spiritual life of children and concluded that our young people are asking the same eternal spiritual questions as thinkers like Tolstoy and Gauguin: "Where do we come from? Who are we? Where are we going?" In the words of one young person, "You have to find something to believe in; you can't just say it's all nothing out there."[2]

The missing ingredient in most of our efforts with young people at risk has been the spiritual dimension. John DiIulio has described the "Three Ms" for effective youth crime and substance abuse prevention:

> Some delinquent kids, like truants and petty thieves, are in need of *monitoring* by a dedicated, caring adult. Others are more criminally involved, and need responsible adults in their lives on a deeper, more intensified level, helping them with their personal problems. They need *mentoring*. But there are others who are among the nation's most

severely at-risk children. Their badly broken lives' spirits cry out for a type and a degree of adult help that is holistic, personal and challenging. They need *ministering*.[3]

In attempting to affect change in a young person's behavior, we must understand what is at the root of their actions. The following diagram illustrates how the observable behavior of a youth is influenced by overarching but less visible factors including attitudes, values, and faith. Comprehensive approaches attempt to target all four, realizing that the deeper one goes, the more powerful the intervention.

LEVELS OF INTERVENTION

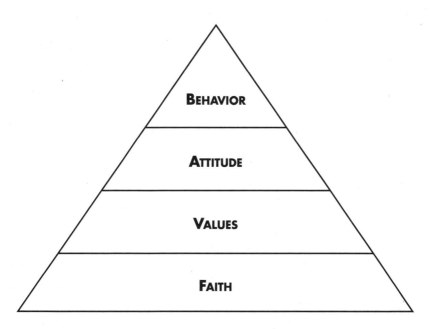

Working With Youth at the Level of Behavior

The majority of juvenile treatment programs focus on the behavioral portion of the equation. B. F. Skinner developed the major components of behavior modification theory. In it, a combination of rewards and punishment is used to influence children to change their behavior from inappropriate to appropriate. According to Skinner, if positive stimuli are given for good behavior, more good behavior will result.

In general it works, for most youth quickly adapt to the expectations of structured program settings, exhibiting exemplary behavior. The problem occurs, however, when youth are released from such programs, and the mechanisms that so faithfully and consistently enforced the new behavior are removed as well. For example, Boys Town conducted many research studies showing that it was not enough to simply modify superficial behavior, for these changes usually did not generalize to situations outside of the artificial reward-and-punishment system.

The superficiality of changes that are externally imposed is readily apparent when a delinquent youth nears his release from a juvenile facility. His whole demeanor begins to change; a hardness overtakes his eyes. He has adapted to his surroundings but knows that what he has learned in the program does not translate well into the world he is soon to reenter. It is not surprising that he quickly returns to previous actions. There has been no real change within the heart or mind. As the sayings go: "A dog returns to its vomit," and "a sow that is washed goes back to her wallowing in the mud."[4]

Surprisingly, most "religious" approaches also tend to deal with troubled youth primarily at the behavior level. If we can just get them to change how they behave, we believe we have succeeded. This is not a new approach. Both Jesus and the Torah attack those who simply go through the motions as being hypocritical if their hearts are not transformed.

Working With Youth at the Level of Attitude

The adult who says "You better change your attitude!" is recognizing that our inner life affects our outer behavior. Psychologists who recognized the narrowness of behavioral approaches have added *thoughts* and *feelings* to the equation. A number of these "cognitive" and "affective" programs address distortions in thinking and problems of self-esteem. The goal is to try to give youth more positive self-messages and to manage their feelings, particularly anger.

Because much behavior is influenced by thoughts and feelings, attention to these factors can make interventions more powerful. However, neither behavior nor thinking fully address the heart of the matter. We can exhort our youth to change their actions or attitudes and control their tempers, but doing so may take more than a simple act of will on their part if they are enmeshed in a lifestyle based on self-centered or antisocial values.

Working With Youth at the Level of Values

An even bolder approach is to focus on how a person's values and philosophy of life directly influence his or her thoughts and actions. These value-based approaches are being used effectively to challenge our youths' commitment to delinquent or drug culture values. For example, pre- and post-testing of youth in peer helping programs at Starr Commonwealth show that most move from delinquent to prosocial values during the course of their treatment. Such programs are sometimes referred to as "therapeutic communities" because they use peer concern and peer accountability as the primary methods for creating change.[5]

Moral development training and various character education programs also seek to instill enduring human virtues and values such as respect, responsibility, and caring for others. An example is the Alcoholics Anonymous (AA) model. Such programs have been shown to make significant positive changes in the lives of many young people. But any serious discussion of values inevitably turns to deeper spiritual questions about the purpose and meaning of life. These are what most powerfully shape our values.

Working With Youth at the Level of Faith

Interventions at this level help youth understand how their theology—their view of God—informs every other area of their lives and gives meaning to their existence. This has been the missing element in youth work in recent years. Yet there is no deeper belief that any of us can hold than our personal understanding of God.

Even agnostics and atheists search for something beyond themselves, even if it is ideologies or material things. And it is that which we hold highest (our *higher power* as AA has termed it) that most greatly influences everything else. Seventeenth-century theologian and president of Princeton University Jonathan Edwards stated, "We always act on our strongest beliefs." And for many people, spiritual convictions are the strongest of their beliefs.

So how is this issue best handled in the context of a secular treatment facility? It is certainly not our recommendation that public schools and juvenile facilities try to become churches. That would be a grave mistake. Neither can we present simplistic approaches to meeting the needs of youth by assuming that the only issues in a troubled young person are spiritual. Rather, we acknowledge that the needs are critical and complex, and effective intervention needs to encompass every dimension of a young person's life, including the spiritual domain.

From Rage to Redemption

Marcus was a youth whose life from the early years seemed devoid of a purpose for living. He was abused at 5, raging at 12, and spent his teen years in prison. His story is a tortuous journey from rage to redemption.

Reared in conflict and instability, Marcus was passed back and forth between parents who had little time for him. He decided early on that he was unwanted and unlovable. He remembers at age 5 wearing a white martial arts outfit, standing proudly beside his father, the instructor of his karate class. It would be only a few years later that his father would use his combat skills to angrily attack his son. "You think you're a man, I'll show you what a man is!" was the last thing Marcus heard before being knocked unconscious.

The main lessons Marcus learned from his father were to hate white people and to distrust the establishment. This kept Marcus from calling child protection authorities. The only safe moments in his life were the brief times he stayed with his grandmother.

A Child Without a Conscience?

At age 11, Marcus began moving around the country with his father and a group of men, many of whom had criminal records. Along the way, Marcus was befriended by a young woman who then seduced and repeatedly abused him sexually. At age 12, he was sent back to his mother and school, raging from rejection and abuse. A police officer who knew him at that time said, "Marcus was violence waiting to happen."

Placed back in middle school, the undisciplined Marcus would accept no correction. Instead, he provoked violent confrontations with his teachers. Sometimes he exploded into such fury that even the school security staff feared him. They would remove the other students from the class instead of Marcus and then call the police to take him away.

At age 14, he was expelled from school and lived on the streets. Hungry for affection, he attached himself to a woman 20 years older than he, also a street person. Although she had an older male companion, soon she and Marcus were in an intimate relationship. The triangle led to a confrontation by the older suitor, who was drunk and violent. In the fray, the man fell and hit his head on the concrete. He died as Marcus tried to revive him.

Arrested and jailed, Marcus warred with his wardens. He was sent to a psychiatric hospital but escaped. Back in jail, a court psychologist tried to interview him, but Marcus was too belligerent. In the evaluation, he described Marcus as a sociopath without a conscience. Marcus was convicted as an adult for manslaughter and aggravated assault and sentenced to serve 8 years.

At age 15, Marcus was transferred to an adult prison. Fearing brutalization by the older prisoners, he coped by attacking before he could be attacked. He quickly earned the reputation as a "crazy kid with heart," because such violent courage is respected in prison. He was actively involved in a prison gang and even participated in an abortive riot, which further increased his status among prisoners.

Every year, Marcus was brought before the parole board, shackled in handcuffs and leg irons. The angry relatives of his victim were always there, demanding that this "animal" not be turned free. Marcus would reciprocate the anger. Once he had to be dragged from the room after confronting the head of the parole board. Adult prisons are not equipped to treat troubled teens, and so Marcus would spend years locked in "the hole."

The Memory of Love

The only stable person in his life had been an elderly grandmother he had occasionally stayed with as a child. Now in prison, the only light in the darkness was from letters sent by his grandmother. She told him not to give up hope, that some day when he got out, he would get married, and that she would help take care of his children. When Marcus was 18, he learned that she was dying. Unable to visit her, he was allowed to record a videotape of himself for her. She wrote back saying that she played it over and over to cheer herself.

When his grandmother died a few weeks later, Marcus became suicidal. He saved his antidepressants and tried to overdose, but failed. Repeatedly, he would slash his wrists and arms, but only ended up with long rows of scars. With the death of his grandmother, Marcus lost any purpose for living.

Locked in the desolate world of solitary confinement, Marcus reached out for distant memories of his grandmother. He tried to recall the love and the lessons she had given to him. A particular incident kept running through his mind:

When I was only 8, I got in a fight with another boy and went crying to my grandmother. She sat me down and told me that the Bible says we should forgive those who hurt us and love our enemies. She tried to show me that God wants us to be peacemakers. I trusted what Grandmother said, so I went out to find my little enemy. I told him that I didn't want to fight him anymore because God wanted me to be his peacemaker. He just beat me up worse than before.

As he recalled that time, Marcus suddenly was struck with the realization that he had become exactly like that boy who had attacked him when he came in peace. Marcus despised himself and felt remorse.

The seed planted so many years earlier began to take root. Marcus became active in the prison church. He had to endure the insults of former gang friends, who mocked those who attended the prison chapel with demeaning slurs. Marcus spent many hours talking with the chaplain. He began to approach fellow prisoners in a new way. He would watch out for younger youth new to the prison and try to guide them away from violence and victimization. Marcus also quit battling guards, and in time, the officers could see that his change was genuine.

Making Amends

In his final parole hearing, Marcus finally apologized to the family of his victims, and they in turn wished him well in rebuilding his life. At age 21, he was finally to be released and paroled to the custody of a stable uncle in another state. The chaplain asked us to work with Marcus during the months before his release, to prepare him for new life. Marcus realized that the strategies he used to survive in prison now must be reversed. He must learn whom to trust rather than automatically distrusting everyone. In conflict, he had to learn to communicate rather than intimidate.

It took many visits with Larry Brendtro before Marcus would dare shed any tears—and only then in the safety of a private visiting room. Marcus explained, "Prison taught me never to cry because you can't afford to have any feelings." But on that spring morning when he was released, he recalls, "I looked at the sky, and trees, and the birds. Then I broke into tears."

"Will I ever be free?"

Marcus has called several times to report on how his life is going. At first, he was desperately afraid that people who learned he was in prison would reject him. "Will I ever be free, or will they always see me as a prisoner?" he asked. The answer is still being decided. Sometimes Marcus becomes very lonely for his friends from the prison church, for the bond that develops between those who share great danger and a common enemy is not the same as the bond that most experience in church "on the outside."

Marcus prays that he will not always feel like an outsider in his outside church. In prison, his church was the most accepting place Marcus had ever known. The pastor had told Marcus that he was like the Saint Dysmas of early Christian tradition. This was the name given to the penitent thief who was crucified beside Jesus. Dysmas also had wounds on his hands and in his heart but was welcomed by Jesus into the community of saints.

Who will welcome Marcus? He is now working in a dry-cleaning store and hoping someday to have enough money to go back to school. He is trying to put his past behind him and is hopeful that he will find friends who will accept him despite his wounds. Marcus was proud that the woman who was his supervisor asked him to spend some time with her 12-year-old son, who also was fatherless and had begun to get into trouble. "I don't find many people who know about my record who are willing to trust me like she did," said Marcus. "Her boy looks up to me so I am trying to be a good influence on him," he added.

Marcus has found only a few new friends as he reaches out cautiously to the church. "So far, even on hot Sundays, I wear a wind-breaker during worship to cover my arms. I still am not sure what church members will think if they see the scars on my wrists."

We have no illusions about the struggles that lie ahead for this young person. The Bible does not tell us the ending of the story of the prodigal son either. For all we know, he might have become restless and left home again. But at least the son knows that he always belongs, that if he stumbles, he can come home to the arms of a waiting father.

Research on Spiritual Development

Youth professionals can no longer afford to remain illiterate about the moral and spiritual dimensions of youth development. Personal belief systems permeate our classrooms in essays, journals, and discussions of current events and controversial topics. Therapists and youth workers also encounter spiritual issues unless they make them unwelcome. Even academics and scientists are entering the spiritual domain as shown by the following examples:

- Studies of high-risk Hawaiian children by resilience researchers Werner and Smith found that spiritual faith is positively related to successful life adjustment. Similar findings on Black and Hispanic persons are cited in this study.[6] Many persons from troubled backgrounds attribute their turnaround to a religious commitment.

- James Garbarino cites research that shows that being spiritually anchored reduces substance abuse, depression, suicide, casual sex. It also helps youth overcome trauma.[7]

- Robert Freedman, at the University of Chicago, conducted a comprehensive study and concluded that young people who are active in church are more likely to finish school, avoid out-of-wedlock pregnancies, and stay out of trouble with the law. This was further confirmed by the findings of Harvard University economist Richard Freeman, who said, "The surest guarantee that an African-American urban youth will not fall to drugs or crime is regular church attendance."[8]

- Medical researcher Herbert Benson documents links between spirituality and health.[9] Prayer alters the brain functioning, moving it to a peaceful mode which is the opposite of the fight-or-flight response. Because a hunger for faith exists in all cultures, the brain is probably "hard wired" to develop spiritual beliefs that make human existence meaningful.

The Levels of Spiritual Development

A number of prominent researchers in spiritual development have studied how faith develops in children and adults. Like moral development levels, researchers believe the following process is common across a wide range of cultural situations and faith traditions.

Stage 1: Selfish and unprincipled. Children begin as egocentric and do not live for any cause beyond themselves. If they do not advance beyond this stage, they will likely gravitate to correctional or treatment settings. Some escape into substance abuse or suicide. Often a crisis sparks a conversion to stage two.

Stage 2: Committed believers. Having moved from self-centered thinking, they are able to find an external source of power. They draw strength from predictable forms of worship and turn to God for peace and protection.

Stage 3: Spiritual doubters. With adolescence or independence, youth may rebel against the authority of their childhood religion and parental teachings. Some leave the church but others remain, lacking a strong religious commitment. They may keep ethical principles, and many who search deeply for truths will in time reclaim a faith tradition and move to stage four.

Stage 4: Return to spirituality. These persons have moved beyond their doubts and rebellion to become deeply connected to God. They have been able to integrate their spirituality with other areas of life.

It should be emphasized that not all youth go through the doubting stage to the point of rejecting religious beliefs.

However, it will be reassuring to many parents that doubting in adolescence is often a temporary stage. With more life experience, many young people return to the faith of their fathers and mothers. In fact, one survey of people who possessed vibrant faith 10 years *after* high school discovered two common denominators: first, they were raised in an environment where they saw authentic faith lived out; and second, they rebelled against it for a time. Not just confined to adolescence, a life crisis at any age can have the positive effect of strengthening one's faith.

The Other Prodigal Son

Early in this book we examined the story of the prodigal son who came from a solid family with loving parents. We now look at another prodigal in Scripture, one whose life and background are the opposite of the one Jesus told about.

The Apostle Paul penned a short letter to his friend, Philemon, a very well-to-do man from the city of Colossae in Asia Minor. One of Philemon's slaves had apparently stolen some money from him and was now on the run. This runaway slave, Onesimus, made it all the way to Rome, more than 1,000 miles from his hometown. It was in this metropolitan city of 1.5 million people that Paul encountered the young fugitive. Like the boy in Luke's gospel, Onesimus found himself far from home in a "strange and distant land."

Less Than a Person

Onesimus' background was the antithesis of the wealthy lad in Jesus' parable. Onesimus was a slave, one of 60 million living in the Roman Empire in the middle of the first century. Belonging to the lowest class in the Roman world, a slave was considered less than a person. Rather, they were things, mere property. Being born a slave almost certainly meant dying as a slave. It was nearly impossible to break out of this class. Many of today's at-risk youths find themselves in much the same predicament, as did the prodigal son who had squandered his birthright. Any status he had previously enjoyed was now gone.

Though Onesimus and the prodigal son came from divergent backgrounds, their similarities far outweigh their differences. And they both have much in common with today's troubled young people. First, the two young men were approximately the same age. Onesimus was likely in his late teens when Paul penned this letter, as was the prodigal son.

Second, both carried a negative societal stigma. The prodigal son, though raised in a wealthy Jewish home, found himself among Gentiles (evidenced by the fact that he was feeding pigs). He must surely have faced the sobering reality of prejudice. Why else would such a capable, hardworking young man find himself starving to death?

Onesimus' stigma was even greater. He and other runaway slaves were branded by a hot iron with the letter F (meaning fugitive) on their foreheads. Many of today's troubled youths are branded in other ways. Though today's troubled youths do not wear a visible brand, they carry the scars of people's statements. Such phrases as "slow learner," "troublemaker," "loser," and "you'll be just like your father" are not easily shed.

For those young people unfortunate enough to have a run-in with the law, the "branding" can go even deeper. Today's young offenders live with their criminal records long after their sentences are served. For example, many states have laws that ban teens with past records from even attending public high schools and colleges. This virtually eliminates them from having access to the education services afforded others—even when they do turn their lives around.

Third, both were on the run. The prodigal son was doomed to the life of an outcast. In a strange land, he could not even provide for his most basic sustenance. For Onesimus, it was worse yet. Once caught, his punishment would likely be death. Many of today's high-risk kids live with the same hopelessness. Alone and abandoned, their lives seem doomed to destruction, and many are convinced they will not live to be 21 years of age, a self-fulfilling prophecy for some.

Fourth, someone intervened in their lives. Without the aid of an outside person, there was no hope for either one, for society was certainly not willing to give them a second chance. In the case of the prodigal son, the father ran ahead of the community of judges to avert the natural consequences. In the case of Onesimus, the Apostle Paul stepped in. First, he shared his faith with Onesimus, who responded. But then he began to do something much more risky. He started advocating for this young man's freedom, and that was no more popular a stand to take then than it is now.

Taking a Chance

In A.D. 61, probably just a few months before Paul wrote Philemon on behalf of Onesimus, an incident occurred that shocked all of Rome. The prefect of the city, Pedanius Secundus, was murdered by one of his slaves. Consequently, the Roman Senate voted to enforce a law already on the books. Four hundred of the murderous slave's relatives—men, women, and children known to be innocent of the crime—were put to death. Clearly, this was neither the time nor the place to be advocating for a runaway, delinquent slave. Paul did it anyway.

Advocating for high-risk individuals always involves some sort of risk. The father of the prodigal son endured public humiliation as he ran to receive back his son without so much as a lecture. Surely his neighbors had much to discuss about a gullible old man who knew nothing about responsible child-rearing. In addition, the relationship he had enjoyed with his elder son was now greatly strained. A teenage son rebelled, and now it appeared that the only one suffering was his gracious father. It cost him, both financially and in his public standing.

In the same way, when Paul wrote to Philemon, he was risking his own good reputation on a young thief. He asked his friend to drop all charges against Onesimus, who had stolen from him. And if that were not enough, he then requested that Onesimus be freed from his status as a slave and made a free man. Even more outrageous, he requested that Philemon make Onesimus a brother and an equal!

Paul also put his money where his mouth was. He instructed his friend to charge to him whatever Onesimus owed, saying, "I will pay it back." This kind of request was unheard of in first-century Rome. Was a runaway slave really worth the risk? Apparently, Paul thought so.

We do not know what happened to the prodigal son, but whatever became of Onesimus? The Bible does not say specifically, but some 50 years later, Ignatius, the Bishop of Antioch, wrote a letter about a man who seems to fit the exact description of this runaway slave. Ignatius refers to him as "Onesimus, Bishop of Ephesus"—a key city in the first century. Apparently, Philemon also took a risk and did what Paul had requested. And something even more unlikely than a slave becoming a citizen happened. That slave went on to become the primary pastor in all of Ephesus!

Amazing Grace

This book ends as it began, with stories of various prodigal youth in our world. Some come from families of means, while others have nothing. Some have families they can return to, while others only dream of such things. Though their backgrounds may be vastly different, their needs are the same. We meet our modern prodigals everywhere—in tenements and mansions, as strangers on the streets, and among our relatives. Our biggest threat and our greatest opportunity are hidden behind their angry, distrustful, and lonely faces.

Connecting to youth in conflict is not a simple task. Still, there is much reason for hope. We now have a considerable body of youth development research about how to help these young persons turn around their lives. In this effort, families, schools, youth organizations, and faith communities all have important contributions to make.

Ultimately, each young person is responsible for his or her own actions. But adults also must shoulder their responsibilities. Only we can ensure that all of our children are provided opportunities to thrive in environments that nurture belonging, mastery, independence, and generosity.

Where do each of us fit in these prodigal stories? Are we like the elder brother of the prodigal, concerned only with banishing young transgressors? Or will we step forward to welcome wayward youth back into our communities, schools, churches, and homes? Our answer depends on deeply personal but often unexamined beliefs.

An early pioneer in youth work, professor Alan Keith-Lucas, once observed that there are two contradictory spiritual mindsets that influence our approach to persons who violate our values. These mindsets are found among persons of faith as well as those who subscribe to no creed at all. In the metaphor of Dr. Keith-Lucas, each of us either acts like God's probation officer who sets out to stomp out sin or as a forgiven sinner who reaches out to brothers and sisters in need of redemption.

Perhaps personal brokenness is the best preparation for a spirit of redemption, for it brings home the reality that each of us is in need of grace. Grace is the gift of forgiveness to one who does not deserve such generosity. Grace is also what our troubled youth need the most.

Few should understand the spirit of forgiveness better than persons of faith. After all, it was a former murderer, Moses, who was chosen to lead Israel from captivity and to bring the Ten Commandments to people of the world. Paul of Tarsus, another murderer and a perpetrator of hate crimes, authored much of the New Testament. Saint Augustine felt compelled to publish a book of confessions to chronicle his years of youthful delinquencies. The composer Vivaldi formed a magnificent choir of young girls who had once been prostitutes to perform his stirring sacred music. Ship captain John Newton made his fortune as a racist slave trader, but would later write the powerful hymn of redemption, "Amazing Grace," in 1779.

Perhaps the most neglected of teachings by Jesus was that his followers visit outcasts and prisoners. Even the word "visit" is a weak translation. In its original Greek, the verb is *episkeptomai*, which actually means "to spend time with and to establish close bonds." It is the same word used to describe God's reclaiming relationship with his errant children. As stated through the prophet Hosea, "It was I who healed them. I led them with cords of human kindness, with ties of love."[10] Or, in the words of John Newton's hymn,

> Amazing grace, how sweet the sound,
> That saved a wretch like me!
> I once was lost but now am found,
> Was blind, but now I see.

Appendixes

Covenant of Commitment

STRAIGHT AHEAD MINISTRIES
COVENANT OF COMMITMENT

1. I'm asking you to love me enough to tell me the truth about myself as you see it.
   "Wounds from a friend can be trusted, but an enemy multiplies kisses." (Proverbs 27:6)
2. I love you enough to commit to confronting you about things I'm concerned about in your life.
   "Better is open rebuke than hidden love." (Proverbs 27:5)
3. I give you permission to ask me questions about anything you're concerned about in my life.
   "Let a righteous man strike me—it is a kindness; let him rebuke me—it is oil on my head. [I] will not refuse it." (Psalm 141:5)
4. I trust you, that the things you tell me will be in my best interest and out of love for me.
   "As iron sharpens iron, so one man sharpens another." (Proverbs 27:17)

Signed:

_____   _____

_____   _____

_____   _____

ACCOUNTABILITY QUESTIONS

1. How have you been doing recently in areas of temptation like drugs, alcohol, sex, or foul language?
2. How has your attitude been this week toward family, work, friends, and self?
3. Is there somebody you need to forgive or ask to forgive you?
4. How has your time with God been this week? What has been your experience with prayer, Bible reading, and spending time alone?
5. What kinds of negative things have you allowed into your mind this week? (Think about the impact of music, movies, TV, magazines, and peers.)
6. Is there any area in which you think God is asking you to take another step?

40 Developmental Assets

 Search Institute has identified the following building blocks of healthy development that help young people grow up healthy, caring, and responsible.

CATEGORY   ASSET NAME AND DEFINITION

EXTERNAL ASSETS

SUPPORT

1. **Family support**—Family life provides high levels of love and support.
2. **Positive family communication**—Young person and her or his parent(s) communicate positively, and young person is willing to seek advice and counsel from parent(s).
3. **Other adult relationship**—Young person receives support from three or more non-parent adults.
4. **Caring neighborhood**—Young person experiences caring neighbors.
5. **Caring school climate**—School provides a caring, encouraging environment.
6. **Parent involvement in schooling**—Parent(s) are actively involved in helping young person succeed in school.

CATEGORY   ASSET NAME AND DEFINITION

EXTERNAL ASSETS

EMPOWERMENT

7. **Community values youth**—Young person perceives that adults in the community value youth.
8. **Youth as resources**—Young people are given useful roles in the community.
9. **Service to others**—Young person serves in the community one hour or more per week.
10. **Safety**—Young person feels safe at home, at school, and in the neighborhood.

BOUNDARIES & EXPECTATIONS

11. **Family boundaries**—Family has clear rules and consequences and monitors the young person's whereabouts.
12. **School boundaries**—School provides clear rules and consequences.
13. **Neighborhood boundaries**—Neighbors take responsibility for monitoring young people's behavior.
14. **Adult role models**—Parent(s) and other adults model positive, responsible behavior.
15. **Positive peer influence**—Young person's best friends model responsible behavior.
16. **High expectations**—Both parent(s) and teachers encourage the young person to do well.

CONSTRUCTIVE USE OF TIME

17. **Creative activities**—Young person spends three or more hours per week in lessons or practice in music, theater, or other arts.
18. **Youth programs**—Young person spends three or more hours per week in sports, clubs, or organizations at school and/or in the community.
19. **Religious community**—Young person spends one or more hours per week in activities in a religious institution.
20. **Time at home**—Young person is out with friends "with nothing special to do" two or fewer nights per week.

CATEGORY   ASSET NAME AND DEFINITION

INTERNAL ASSETS

COMMITMENT TO LEARNING	21. **Achievement motivation**—Young person is motivated to do well in school. 22. **School engagement**—Young person is actively engaged in learning. 23. **Homework**—Young person reports doing at least one hour of homework every school day. 24. **Bonding to school**—Young person cares about her or his school. 25. **Reading for pleasure**—Young person reads for pleasure three or more hours per week.
POSITIVE VALUES	26. **Caring**—Young person places high value on helping other people. 27. **Equality and social justice**—Young person places high value on promoting equality and reducing hunger and poverty. 28. **Integrity**—Young person acts on convictions and stands up for her or his beliefs. 29. **Honesty**—Young person "tells the truth even when it is not easy." 30. **Responsibility**—Young person accepts and takes personal responsibility. 31. **Restraint**—Young person believes it is important not to be sexually active or to use alcohol or other drugs.
SOCIAL COMPETENCIES	32. **Planning and decision making**—Young person knows how to plan ahead and make choices. 33. **Interpersonal competence**—Young person has empathy, sensitivity, and friendship skills. 34. **Cultural competence**—Young person has knowledge of and comfort with people of different cultural/racial/ethnic backgrounds. 35. **Resistance skills**—Young person can resist negative peer pressure and dangerous situations. 36. **Peaceful conflict resolution**—Young person seeks to resolve conflict nonviolently.

CATEGORY   ASSET NAME AND DEFINITION

INTERNAL ASSETS	**POSITIVE IDENTITY**	37. **Personal power**—Young person feels he or she has control over "things that happen to me."
		38. **Self-esteem**—Young person reports having a high self-esteem.
		39. **Sense of purpose**—Young person reports that "my life has a purpose."
		40. **Positive view of personal future**—Young person is optimistic about her or his personal future.

A Life Space Crisis Intervention

One progressive model of reconciliation is to use a crisis in a youth's life as an opportunity for that youth to develop his or her resilience and learn how to cope with life's challenges. The Life Space Crisis Intervention provides a roadmap for talking to youth in crisis.

The Life Space Crisis Intervention (LSCI) is built around the conflict cycle. Developed by Mary Wood and Nicholas Long, LSCI turns a natural problem in the "life space" of participants into a teaching opportunity. Although advanced training and certification is available for teachers, principals, counselors, pastors, and others who want advanced skills, any thoughtful person can learn the foundation skills of LSCI.

In LSCI, the adult becomes a coach and the youth in conflict becomes the expert. The adult is not trying to find out what is wrong with the youth, but is helping him or her use strengths and intelligence to solve problems. It is presented here in a simple, abbreviated, four-step format:

1. Defusing the conflict

2. Building a time line of the conflict

3. Understanding what causes the conflict

4. Resolving the conflict

Following is a summary of our LSCI with Kim and her parents, as was discussed in Chapter 9.

The Crisis Situation

Kim was raised in a very loving family, but her issues with authority, combined with her rocky relationships with peers, were causing tremendous stress. While both parents were well educated, her father's military academy background and parental style only served to heighten the tension. Kim's strong-spirited nature drew her into more and more negative behavior. When she began smoking, partying, and hanging out with boys who were several years older, the clashes with her parents became more frequent and hostile.

Kim's mother was losing her position in a company that was downsizing, so she became too emotionally drained to even enter the conflict and retreated into depression. Soon all positive communication in the family came to a halt. Out of desperation, her parents threatened to have her removed from the home if she did not change her behavior.

This made matters worse, and Kim rebelled against her parents even more. If she felt the least bit guilty for all the pain and disappointment she was causing them, she certainly did not let them know. Instead, she intentionally defied all the values her parents had tried to instill in her.

After Kim ran away for the second time, her father notified the police. By now, the entire family was overcome with self-defeating behavior. By trying to overpower his daughter, the father ended up having no influence over her at all. By retreating into her depression, her mother severed all the bonds she previously had with her daughter. By fighting her parents, Kim cut herself off from the love and support she needed.

Kim and her family could not get out of this mess alone. When they sat down together, their "family meetings" ended in accusations and explosions. They needed help in sorting out their conflict if reconciliation was to occur.

Larry Brendtro received a call from Kim's desperate parents and explains what happened. She had run away again the night before and upon returning home, the war had begun all over again. Her mother was crying and her father was trying to call officials at the detention center, but nobody saw this domestic conflict as their battle.

Out of fear that Kim would run right out the door again, her mother asked if the three of them could come to the office on Saturday afternoon to talk. Using threats of detention to get Kim to come created further anger in Kim. This was the problem. Now how could we make it an opportunity?

1. Defusing the Conflict

Goal: Before problem solving can begin, we must defuse strong emotions and lure the child back into communication. The first step in calming down a youth is for the adult to be in control of his or her own emotions and avoid becoming moralistic or judgmental. The goal is simply to help the young person become more composed so that we can focus on what happened.

The tone of the family's mood was hostile and defensive. The father ranted about Kim's behavior, about how she lied, how she disrespected her mother, how she smoked, and hung out with wild youth. The previous day she had run away from home again and, when she came back in the morning, her attitude was still rotten. As her father went on and on, her mother mostly sat and cried. Kim sat with her arms crossed, in stony silence, furious about having to be there. Once we felt we had a general idea of the problem, we decided it would be easier to defuse the conflict by separating the generations. My wife Janna took the parents and went through a process similar to the one I went through with Kim, as described below.

When Kim and I were alone, I suggested we move to more comfortable chairs in the corner. Kim claimed the large recliner, leaving me the granny rocker. This was our dialogue:

> **Larry:** I bet you don't like being dragged here to meet with some counselor.
>
> **Kim:** I hate it; she made me see a counselor in sixth grade when she got divorced.

> **Larry:** If I were forced to see a counselor, I would probably refuse to talk.

Of course, she was probably forced to come today, but by validating her right not to talk, I communicated respect and defused her resistance.

> **Kim:** Well, I had to talk or she wouldn't let me out of her office, so I gave her a bunch of fake problems.

By this point, Kim was calmer, and we were communicating honestly. She shared that she had not been honest with her previous counselor and played games by laying a false scent to keep the counselor confused. She was no longer angry, and we were ready to make the transition to the next stage.

2. Building a Time Line of the Conflict

Goal: Because youth in crisis seldom think logically and sequentially, we want to help them sort out what actually happened. It is seldom helpful to ask them why they did something, which will likely produce a nonanswer such as "Because my parents are jerks." Instead, we ask them to help us understand what really happened. Together we figure out the time line of how the crisis unfolded. Even if the initial version of events seems distorted, we listen respectfully and ask factual, nonblaming questions. We are interested in specific behavior but also in what the youth and others in the crisis might have been thinking or feeling at the time.

> **Larry:** I wonder if you could help me understand what really happened that led to your decision to run away yesterday?

Kim reported that she came home at 4:30 and by 5:30 things were so tense she stormed out the door. As we examined the time line of the events, we saw that her problems actually started in school where she had a physical fight with Carmen, a girl who had been calling her names all week. Carmen had then threatened to get her 18-year-old boyfriend to retaliate. We then digressed to examine the earlier time line of the fight in school, which was a classic conflict cycle. We drew a conflict cycle and traced its escalation:

1. *Stress*: Another girl called her names in front of friends.

2. *Feelings*: "I got mad."

3. *Behavior*: "I called her names back."

4. *Reaction*: "She called me more names."

After we followed the incident through two escalating cycles, she said: "I've got to figure out how to quit going in circles with her." Then we returned to the time line of the original conflict with her mother. "After school," she shared, "I was so upset I drove around an hour, smoking before coming home." When she got home, another conflict cycle erupted between Kim and her mother. We then reconstructed the sequence of those events.

1. *Stress:* Kim came home smelling of smoke, and her mother angrily confronted her about smoking.

2. *Feelings:* Kim was already upset from the fight at school, and now she became furious at her mother.

3. *Behavior:* Kim told her mother, "I don't know why you are so picky about my smoking. I heard the kinds of things you did that caused my dad to divorce you."

4. *Reaction:* The mother then had the same furious feelings as Kim. The mother said she had had it with Kim and would send her to a boot camp. Kim felt totally rejected, and in less than an hour after she arrived at home, she was out the door and on the road.

3. Understanding What Causes the Conflict

Goal: Having determined what happened, we are better able to identify the central issue. Sometimes a problem is simple and limited in scope. More often, the immediate problem is the latest in a string of similar problems. A youth can become locked into these patterns of self-defeating behavior. The youth who understands how conflict cycles are created and maintained is in a better position to prevent them in the future.

Every member of this family was ensnared in conflict. Kim loved her mother and was deeply hurt that she wanted to send her away. Kim was rebelling particularly against her father who acted like a military officer, always telling her what to do, but she longed for earlier times when the father and daughter had had fun together. Kim realized she acted as if she did not care about what her parents thought, but she really cared deeply and needed to tell them this and take steps to restore relationships.

In another room, Kim's parents were going through a similar process. The father was becoming able to see how his authoritarian response in the end rendered him powerless over Kim. The mother could see how her depression was triggering conflict cycles with Kim as well. Like their daughter, they did not know how to disengage from the conflict and talk respectfully with one another. After sorting out these feelings, the family was brought back together.

4. Resolving the Conflict

Goal: When people understand how conflicts develop, they are able to find better strategies for coping with such situations. Helping young persons reflect on a problem objectively enables them to see how their behavior has hurt others and what they can do to make amends.

Kim explained to her mother what was really bothering her after school and shared how much it hurt her to feel her parents were giving up on her. Both her mother and father assured Kim of their love for her and assured her that they were not giving up on her. Her mother shared how she had let her own problems from work interfere with home life, just as Kim had brought her problems home from school, and asked Kim to forgive her. In turn, Kim told her mother she was sorry for the mean things she had said and done. Mother and daughter cried and embraced.

Kim then told her father that she was afraid of him and hated how he tried to control her like he was some general. Her father then shared with Kim that she would probably be surprised to know how totally helpless he felt trying to influence her. Kim told her father they used to have so much fun together, and she wanted it to be that way again.

"Well, what should I do when you treat your mother badly?" he asked. Kim's mother then asked her husband not to always come to her defense against Kim, but to let mother and daughter work out any conflicts with one another.

Though it began as a complicated session, as these people who really loved one another shared and apologized to each other, all became tearful and were reconciled. The mother and father told Kim that they wanted to trust her instead of trying to police everything she did. Kim said she hated fighting with them and wanted to do her part to bring harmony back in the house. The family left together.

Several months later, her parents sent a card saying how much more mature and respectful Kim had become. They were continuing to try to work things out instead of getting into conflict cycles. And in the process, they began enjoying one another again, as they had done years earlier. While not all sessions end this well, if difficulties reemerge, this same problem-solving process can be used again.

Resources for Reclaiming Youth

Thousands of organizations worldwide work on behalf of challenging children and youth. The great majority of these are voluntary, faith-based, or non-sectarian initiatives. Following is a sample of such organizations, including many that provide information on their activities through their websites.

Youth Policy Organizations

Alliance for Children and Families
800-221-3726, www.alliance1.org

Child Welfare League of America
202-638-2952, www.cwla.org

Children's Defense Fund
202-628-2952, www.childrensdefense.org

Council for Exceptional Children
888-CEC-SPED, www.cec.sped.org

Advocacy for Families With Challenging Children

Center on Family Support and Children's Mental Health
800-547-8887 x 4040, www.rtc.pdx.edu

Children and Adults With Attention Deficit Disorders (CHADD)
800-233-4050, www.chadd.org

Federation of Families for Children's Mental Health
703-684-7710, www.ffcmh.org

Pacer Center's Behavior Disorder and Juvenile Justice Programs
612-827-2966, www.pacer.org

Prevent Child Abuse America
800-CHILDREN (caller will be routed to the closest state with
an affiliate organization), ncpa@childabuse.org

Youth in Crisis Hotlines

Boys Town USA National Hotline
800-448-3000, www.boystown.org

KidsPeace
800-8KID-123, www.kidspeace.org

Professional Training Resources

American Correctional Association
800-222-5646, www.corrections.com/aca

Boys Town USA National Training Center
800-545-5771, www.boystown.org

The Bureau for at-Risk Youth
800-99-YOUTH, www.at-risk.com

Circle of Courage
888-647-2532, www.reclaiming.com

Developmental Therapy/Teaching Institute
706-369-5689, www.uga.edu/dttp

Discipline with Dignity
800-772-5227, www.disciplineassociates.com

Life Space Crisis Intervention Institute
800-267-1507

LSCI Hotline
301-654-4777

National Educational Service
800-733-6786, www.nesonline.com

National Gang Crime Research Center
773-995-2494

National Resource Center for Youth Services
918-585-2986, www.nrcys.ou.edu

Phi Delta Kappa International Center for Professional
Development
800-766-1156, www.pdkintl.org

Reclaiming Youth International Seminars
800-647-5244, www.reclaiming.com

Starr Commonwealth Training and Resource Center
800-837-5591,
www.starr.org/training/training_resource_center.htm

Walker Trieschman Center
617-769-4008, www.cwla.org/trieschman/walkertrieschman

Community Youth Involvement

Big Brothers/Big Sisters of America
215-567-7000, www.bbbsa.org

Boys and Girls Clubs of America
404-815-5700, www.bgca.org

4-H
800-368-7432, www.4h-usa.org

Men Against Destruction—Defending Against Drugs and
Social Disorder (MAD DADS)
402-451-3500, www.maddadsnational.com

National Service Learning Clearinghouse
800-808-SERVe, www.nicsl.coled.umn.edu

National Black Child Development Institute
800-556-2234, www.nbcdi.org/

Search Institute
800-888-7828, www.search-institute.org

Publishers and Publications

National Educational Service
800-733-6786, www.nesonline.com

Reclaiming Children and Youth Journal
800-897-3202, www.proedinc.com

Reclaiming Youth Library
888-647-2532, www.reclaiming.com

Search Institute
800-888-7828, www.search-institute.org

Youth Today
800-319-9450, www.youthtoday.org

Positive Peer-Group Cultures

Bullying Prevention
888-647-2532

Educators for Social Responsibility
800-370-2515, www.esrnational.org

EQUIP Peer Helping Program
614-292-7918 or 888-647-2532

Strength Based Services International
www.empowerkids.org

Resolving Conflict Creatively Program of Educators
for Social Responsibility
212-509-0022, www.esrnational.org/about-rccp.html

Faith-Based Programs for Challenging Youth

Focus on the Family
800-A-FAMILY, www.family.org

Jewish Children's Bureau
800-879-2522 or 216-932-2800

Pathways: Fostering Spiritual Growth Among At-Risk Youth
(a Boys Town program)
800-545-5771, www.ffbh.boystown.org/NRTC/cntr4adol

Straight Ahead Ministries
508-366-9797, www.straightahead.org

Teen Challenge
800-814-5729, www.teenchallenge.com

International Groups

For groups that are overseas from Canada and the U.S., dial a prefix of 011 before the number.

International Association of Social Educators (AIEJI)
33-320-93-7016

Home-Start International, United Kingdom
44-20-7730-0472 or 44-11-6270-2160

National Association of Child Care Workers, South Africa
www.pretext.co.za/naccw

Youth Aliyah, Israel
972-2-257671

Youth Off the Streets, Australia
61-29692-2420

Endnotes

All Biblical references are taken from The Holy Bible, New International Version, Copyright 1973, 1978, 1984 by International Bible Society, unless otherwise noted.

Chapter 1—Hazards in the World of Children

1. Some of this section contains material given by Mardy Keyes in a lecture entitled "Who Invented Adolescence?" at the Southborough Massachusetts L'Abri on July 16, 1999.

2. Richard Fransen, "With Enough Antagonism, Violence in Schools can Happen Anywhere—Even in Grand Forks," *Dakota Student* (Grand Forks, ND: University of North Dakota, April 27, 1999).

Chapter 2—Reclaiming a Prodigal

1. Kenneth E. Bailey, "The Pursuing Father," *Christianity Today* (October 26, 1998), pages 35-36.

2. Zechariah 3:3–5, the New Jerusalem Bible.

3. Johann Pestalozzi, *The Education of Man* (New York: Philosophical Library, 1951), page 86.

4. Rabindranath Tagore, *Red Oleander* (London: McMillan and Company, 1925), page 64.

Chapter 3—A Rootless Generation

1. National Research Council, Panel on High-Risk Youth, *Losing Generations* (National Academy Press, 1995), page 5.

2. Quote taken from the video *Jesus Is the Answer* (Converse, TX: Go Tell Communications, 1983).

3. David Levy, "Primary Affect Hunger," *American Journal of Psychiatry* (Volume 94, 1937), pages 643–652.

4.   Taken from Nancy R. Gibbs, "Murder in Miniature," reported by Julie Grace & Jon D. Hull, *Time* (September 19, 1994), *Time* archives, www.time.com.

5.   Daniel Patrick Moynihan, *The Negro: The Case for National Action* (Washington DC: Office of Policy, Planning and Research, U.S. Department of Labor, 1965).

6.   David Popenoe, *Life Without Father: Compelling New Evidence that Fatherhood and Marriage Are Indispensable for the Good of Children and Society* (New York: The Free Press, 1996).

7.   Popenoe, *Life Without Father*, pages 142–143.

8.   Cited in Popenoe, *Life Without Father*, page 144.

9.   David Popenoe, "Where's Papa?" *UTNE Reader* (September/October, 1996), page 9.

10. John Snarey, *How Fathers Care for the Next Generation* (Cambridge, MA: Harvard University Press, 1993), pages 163–164.

11. Robert Bly, *Iron John* (Reading, MS: Addison-Wesley, 1990), page 93.

12. Sue Horton, "Mothers, Sons, and the Gangs: When a Gang Becomes Part of the Family," *Los Angeles Times Magazine* (October 16, 1988), page 8.

13. Cited in Deborah Prothrow-Stith & Michaele Weissman, *Deadly Consequences* (New York: HarperCollins Publishers, 1991), page 6.

14. 2 Corinthians 5:14, King James Version.

15. This treatment model is described in Harry Vorrath and Larry Brendtro, *Positive Peer Culture,* 2nd edition (Hawthorne, NY: Aldine du Gruyther, 1985).

16. J. C. Chambers, "Youth Caught in the Enchanting Web of Chemicals," *Reclaiming Children and Youth* (Spring, 1999), pages 34–38.

Chapter 4—The Broken Community

1. Jack and Judith Balswick, *The Family: A Christian Perspective on the Contemporary Home* (Grand Rapids, MI: Baker, 1991), page 133.

2. Linda Lantieri and Janet Patti, *Waging Peace in Our Schools* (Boston: Beacon Press, 1996).

3. Phi Delta Kappa Commission on Discipline, *Handbook for Developing Schools with Good Discipline* (Bloomington, IN: Phi Delta Kappa, 1982).

4. Herbert L. Needleman, Julie A. Riess, Michael J. Tobin, Gretchen E. Biesecker, & Joel B. Greenhouse, "Bone Lead Levels and Delinquent Behavior," *Journal of the American Medical Association* (February 7, 1996), pages 363–369, 403.

5. Lili Garfinkel, "Children With Disabilities in the Justice System," *Reclaiming Children and Youth* (Summer 1998), pages 80–82.

6. Personal communication with the author Larry Brendto.

7. Frederick Thrasher, *The Gang* (Chicago: University of Chicago Press, 1927), pages 72–75.

8. William I. Thomas, *The Unadjusted Girl: A Study of Prostitutes, Runaways, and Maladjusted Girls* (Boston: Little, Brown, and Company, 1923), pages 4–38.

9. Acts 2:44–46, New Revised Standard Version.

Chapter 5—Pathways to Trouble

1. Martin Gold, *Delinquent Behavior in an American City* (Belmont, CA: Brooks/Cole Publishing Company, 1970).

2. Stephen Biddulph, *Raising Boys: Why Boys Are Different and How to Help Them Become Happy and Well-Balanced Men* (Sydney, Australia: Finch Publishing, 1997).

3. Martin Strommen, *Five Cries of Youth* (New York: Harper and Row, 1979).

4. John Hoover & Ronald Oliver, *The Bullying Prevention Handbook: A Guide for Principals, Teachers, and Counselors* (Bloomington, IN: National Educational Service, 1996), page 3.

5. Hoover & Oliver, *The Bullying Prevention Handbook,* page 14.

6. James Garbarino, *Lost Boys: Why Our Sons Turn Violent and How We Can Save Them* (New York: Free Press, 1999), page 128.

7. Adam Rogers, Pat Wingert, & Thomas Hayde, "Why the Young Kill," *Newsweek* (May 3, 1999), page 35.

8. David Fassler, *Help Me, I'm Sad,* cited in Howard Chua-Eoan, "Escaping from the Darkness," *Time* (May 31, 1999), page 47.

9. Albert Trieschman & Bernard Levine, "Helping Children Learn to Deal with Sadness," in James Whittaker and Albert Trieschman (Editors), *Children Away From Home* (Chicago: Aldine-Atherton, 1972).

10. Howard Chua-Eoan, "Escaping from the Darkness," *Time* (May 31, 1999), page 44.

11. Ann Imse, "Sick Kids Behind Bars," *Denver Rocky Mountain News* (February 28, 1999), page 7A.

12. John Cloud, "Just a Routine School Shooting," *Time* (May 31, 1999), pages 36–37.

Chapter 6—Courage for the Discouraged

1. Excerpted from *The American Heritage® Dictionary of the English Language,* 3rd Edition (Boston: Houghton Mifflin Company, 1996).

2. 1 Thessalonians 2:11–12.

3. The Circle of Courage name and drawing by George Bluebird is trademark protected. Reproduction is granted for noncommercial, educational purposes only by Reclaiming Youth International, Lennox, South Dakota.

4. Henri Nouwen, *The Return of the Prodigal Son* (New York: Doubleday, 1992).

5. Proverbs 22:6.

6. "Fat Phobia in the Fijis: TV-Thin Is In," *Newsweek* (May 31, 1999), page 70.

7. *The Troubled Journey* (Minneapolis, MN: Search Institute, 1990).

Chapter 7—Reparenting

1. Michael Petit and Thomas R. Brooks, "Abuse and Delinquency: Two Sides of the Same Coin," *Reclaiming Children and Youth* (Summer, 1998), pages 77–79.

2. Dorothy Otnow Lewis, M. Feldman, & A. Barrengos, "Violent Juvenile Delinquents: Psychiatric, Neurological, Psychological and Abuse Factors," *Journal of the American Academy of Child Psychiatry* (1979), pages 307–319.

3. I. Schulman, "Delinquents." In S. R. Slavson (Ed.), *The Fields of Group Psychotherapy* (New York: John Wiley and Sons, 1952).

4. "National Early Teen Survey" conducted in 1998 by KidsPeace, Inc. of Orefield, PA.

5. Samuel Read Hall, *Lectures on School-Keeping* (Boston: Richardson, Lord and Hollbrook, 1829), page 47.

6. Taken from a speech given by Peter Benson of the Search Institute at a Black Hills Seminar (October 2, 1998).

7. Linda Nielson, *Adolescence: A Contemporary View*, 3rd Edition (Fort Worth, TX: Harcourt Brace College Publishers, 1996), page 350.

8. 1 Corinthians 4:15.

9. Malachi 4:6.

10. Richard Curwin, "The Bar Mitzvah Gift," *Reclaiming Children and Youth* (Fall 1996), pages 140–142.

11. Denis Stott, *Delinquency and Human Nature* (Dunfermline, Fife, UK: Carnegie United Kingdom Trust, 1950).

12. Scott Larson, *At Risk: Bringing Hope to Hurting Teenagers* (Loveland, CO: Group Publishing, 1999), pages 23–25.

Chapter 8—Redirecting

1. Alan Paton, *Diepkloof: Reflections of Diepkloof Reformatory* (Capetown, South Africa: Credo Press, 1986).

2. Emmy Werner and Ruth Smith, *Overcoming the Odds* (Ithaca, NY: Cornell University Press, 1992).

3. Personal comment made by John Seita to Larry Brendtro.

4. John Seita & Tyrone Baines, "Raising the Rest of the Neighborhood," *Reclaiming Children and Youth* (Spring 1999), page 29.

5. John Gibbs, Granville Potter, and Arnold Goldstein, *The EQUIP Program* (Champaign, IL: Research Press, 1995).

6. Adapted from John Gibbs, Bud Potter, Arnold Goldstein, & Larry Brendtro, "Equipping Youth with Mature Moral Judgment," *Reclaiming Children and Youth* (Spring, 1996), pages 156–162.

7. Thomas Lickona, "Sex Education for the Neglected Heart," *Reclaiming Children and Youth* (Spring, 1998), pages 9–17.

8. Merton Strommen, *Five Cries of Youth* (New York: Harper and Row, 1979).

9. Polly Nichols, "Lessons on Lookism," *Reclaiming Children and Youth* (Summer, 1996), pages 118–122.

10. Myra Sadker & David Sadker, *Failing at Fairness* (New York: C. Scribner's Sons, 1994), page 9.

11. N. Rutstein, *Racism: Unraveling the Fear* (Washington, DC: Global Classroom, 1997).

12. Fritz Redl & David Wineman, *Children Who Hate: The Disorganization and Breakdown of Behavior Controls* (Glencoe, IL: Free Press, 1951).

13. John Gibbs, Granville Potter, and Arnold Goldstein, *The EQUIP Program* (Champaign, IL: Research Press, 1995).

14. Anecdote adapted from a speech by Peter Benson.

15. Waln Brown, *The Other Side of Delinquency* (New Brunswick, NJ: Rutgers University Press, 1983).

Chapter 9—Reconciling

1. Adapted from Fritz Redl & David Wineman's work by Larry Brendtro & Nicholas Long, "Punishment Rituals: Superstition in an Age of Science," *Reclaiming Children and Youth* (Fall, 1999), page 134.

2. Michael Montgomery, "The Powerlessness of Punishment: Angry Pride and Delinquent Identity," *Reclaiming Children and Youth* (Spring, 1997), pages 162–166.

3. Robert R. Martinson, "What Works—Questions and Answers about Prison Reform," *The Public Interest* (1974), pages 22–54.

4. Martin Gold & D.W. Osgood, *Personality and Peer Influence in Juvenile Corrections* (Westport, CT: Greenwood, 1992).

5. Exodus 21:24.

6. Psalm 102:19-20.

7. Paraphrased from 1 Corinthians 1:27–28, New Revised Standard Version.

8. Numbers 32:11.

9. Psalm 25:7.

10. Shannon Brownlee, "Inside the Teen Brain," *U.S. News & World Report* (August 9, 1999), pages 46–47.

11. John J. DiIulio, "Preventing Crime, Saving Children: Sticking to the Basics," *The Prosecutor* (November/December, 1997).

12. Tony Rios, "Growing Up in Prison," *Reclaiming Children and Youth* (Fall, 1997), pages 136–137.

13. Ted Gest & Victoria Pope, "Crime Time Bomb," *U.S. News and World Report* (March 25, 1996), page 36.

14. Anatol Rapaport, *Fights, Games and Debates* (Ann Arbor: University of Michigan Press, 1960).

15. Gordon McLean, *Too Young to Die* (Wheaton, IL: Tyndale House Publishers, 1998).

16. Genesis 50:18–21.

17. Matthew 5: 43–44.

18. John Dawson, *Healing America's Wounds* (Ventura, CA: Regal Books, 1994).

19. Charles Colson & Daniel Van Ness, *Convicted* (Westchester, IL: Crossway Books, 1989), pages 45–47.

20. Cited in Michael Battle, *Reconciliation: The Ubuntu Theology of Desmond Tutu* (Cleveland, OH: Pilgrim Press, 1997), page 27.

21. Mary M. Wood & Nicholas J. Long, *Life Space Intervention: Talking with Children and Youth in Crisis* (Austin, TX: PRO-ED Inc., 1991).

22. Jimmy Carter, *Living Faith* (New York: Random House, 1996), page 111.

Chapter 10—Redeeming

1. M. Scott Peck, *Further Along the Road Less Travelled: The Unending Journey Toward Spiritual Growth* (New York: Simon & Schuster, 1993).

2. Robert Coles, *The Spiritual Life of Children* (Boston: Houghton-Mifflin, 1990), page 299.

3. John J. DiIulio, "Preventing Crime, Saving Children: Sticking to the Basics," *The Prosecutor* (November/December, 1997), page 19.

4. 2 Peter 2:22.

5. Larry Brendtro & William Wasmund, "The Peer Culture Model," in Robert Lyman, Steven Prentice-Dunn, and Stewart Gabel (Editors), *Residential and Inpatient Treatment of Children and Adolescents* (New York: Plenum Press, 1989), pages 81–96.

6. Emmy Werner and Ruth Smith, *Overcoming the Odds* (Ithaca, NY: Cornell University Press, 1992).

7. James Garbarino, *Lost Boys: Why Our Sons Turn Violent and How We Can Save Them* (New York: Free Press, 1999).

8. Cited by Joseph P. Shapiro & Andrea R. Wright, "Can Churches Save America?" *U.S. News and World Report* (September 9, 1996), page 50.

9. Herbert Benson, *Timeless Healing* (New York: Scribner, 1996).

10. Hosea 11:3–4.

Index

About the Authors

Scott J. Larson, D. Min., is president of Straight Ahead Ministries, which he cofounded with his wife, Hanne. This organization provides faith-based services for troubled youth in more than 150 facilities for delinquents in 11 states. At the heart of this organization are programs that train volunteers to provide Bible studies and youth leadership development for at-risk youth.

The organization also provides mentoring programs and aftercare homes for youth after their release from prison. The Larsons live in one of these discipleship homes with up to seven boys, helping them prepare for college and careers. Dr. Larson has written three other books, two for youth workers and one for teens, as well as an assessment tool for youth workers. He received his doctorate from Gordon-Conwell Theological Seminary, and his dissertation is titled *The Spiritual Development of At-Risk Youth*. The Larsons are the parents of two children and reside in Westborough, Massachusetts.

For further information on Straight Ahead Ministries, visit their website at www.straightahead.org or call (508) 366-9797.

Larry K. Brendtro, Ph.D., is president of Reclaiming Youth International, a nonprofit organization that provides research and training, with offices in South Dakota and Michigan. He has been a youthworker, teacher, and psychologist, and for 14 years, he headed the Starr Commonwealth Schools, which serve troubled youth and families in Michigan and Ohio. He has been on the faculty of the University of Illinois, Ohio State University, and Augustana College.

Dr. Brendtro's doctorate from the University of Michigan is in education and psychology, and his dissertation focused on youth with problems of conscience. He has authored numerous books on youth in conflict and has trained professionals worldwide. He and Nicholas Long of American University founded the journal *Reclaiming Children and Youth*. In 1994, Dr. Brendtro established the Black Hills Seminars, an international training institute for reclaiming youth. Larry and his wife, Janna, a teacher and editor of youth publications, have three adult children and reside in the Black Hills of South Dakota.

For further information on Reclaiming Youth International, visit the organization's website at www.reclaiming.com or call (800) 647-5244.

About *Reclaiming Our Prodigal Sons and Daughters* and the National Educational Service

The mission of the National Educational Service is to provide tested and proven resources that help those who work with youth create safe and caring schools, agencies, and communities where all children succeed. *Reclaiming Our Prodigal Sons and Daughters* is just one of many resources and staff development opportunities NES provides that focus on building a community circle of caring. If you have any questions, comments, articles, manuscripts, or youth art you would like us to consider for publication, please contact us at the address below. Or visit our website at:

www.nesonline.com

Staff Development Opportunities Include:

Improving Schools through Quality Leadership
Integrating Technology Effectively
Creating Professional Learning Communities
Building Cultural Bridges
Discipline with Dignity
Ensuring Safe Schools
Managing Disruptive Behavior
Reclaiming Youth At Risk
Working with Today's Families

National Educational Service
304 W. Kirkwood Avenue, Suite 2
Bloomington, IN 47404-5132
(812) 336-7700
(800) 733-6786 (toll-free number)
FAX (812) 336-7790
e-mail: nes@nesonline.com
www.nesonline.com

NEED MORE COPIES OR ADDITIONAL RESOURCES ON THIS TOPIC?

Need more copies of this book? Want your own copy? Need additional resources on this topic? If so, you can order additional materials by using this form or by calling us toll free at (800) 733-6786 or (812) 336-7700. Or you can order by FAX at (812) 336-7790, or visit our website at www.nesonline.com.

Title	Price*	Quantity	Total
Reclaiming Our Prodigal Sons and Daughters	$ 18.95		
A MentorActive Approach to Reclaiming Youth at Risk training kit	139.00		
Lessons for Life video set	495.00		
Reclaiming Youth At Risk video set	295.00		
Reclaiming Youth At Risk: Our Hope for the Future	21.95		
What Do I Do When . . . ? How to Achieve Discipline with Dignity	21.95		
Rediscovering Hope: Our Greatest Teaching Strategy	21.95		
Discipline with Dignity for Challenging Youth	24.95		
Discipline with Dignity video set	356.00		
Bullying Prevention Handbook	23.95		
		SUBTOTAL	
		SHIPPING	
Continental U.S.: Please add 5% of order total. Outside continental U.S.: Please add 7% of order total.			
		HANDLING	
Continental U.S.: Please add $3. Outside continental U.S.: Please add $5.			
		TOTAL (U.S. funds)	

*Price subject to change without notice.

❏ Check enclosed   ❏ Purchase order enclosed
❏ Money order   ❏ VISA, MasterCard, Discover, or American Express (circle one)

Credit Card No._____ Exp. Date_____
Cardholder Signature _____

SHIP TO:
First Name_____ Last Name_____
Position _____
Institution Name_____
Address_____
City_____ State_____ ZIP_____
Phone_____ FAX_____
E-mail _____

National Educational Service
304 W. Kirkwood Avenue, Suite 2
Bloomington, IN 47404-5132
(812) 336-7700 • (800) 733-6786 (toll-free number)
FAX (812) 336-7790
e-mail: nes@nesonline.com • www.nesonline.com